# A YEAR OF SUNDAYS

# A YEAR
# OF
# SUNDAYS

## Belinda Jeffery

### with photography by Rodney Weidland

A JULIE GIBBS BOOK

for

SIMON & SCHUSTER
AUSTRALIA

# Contents

# Introduction

Who would have thought it? What started a few years ago
as one little square in a far corner of the internet feels to
have taken on a life of its own. For me, Instagram was
initially a space to dip my toe in the waters of social media,
but as time passed, I realised it was becoming much more.
Although I only post once a week, on a Sunday, I noticed
that I was getting more and more comments from people
about what quickly became known as my 'Sunday Post'.
These have continued to grow over time, and I've been
surprised, touched, and more than a little overwhelmed
by the extraordinary response my posts receive.

   I talk about simple, everyday life – the farmers I know
and the markets I visit; cakes, pies and pythons (in our
case!); cooking and eating, and my cooking classes. And
I make observations about the extraordinary world of nature
that is so much part of my daily life. These posts seem to
have struck a chord with a remarkable number of people.
I've had ongoing chats for years with many of those who
follow my posts, so much so that we almost feel like family.
There's a sense of community and a return to a simpler life
around what I do and what I share.

   The idea that these posts could be brought together in
a book initially came from my followers, as so many have
written and suggested I should do so. The seed was planted
and after niggling away at me for quite some time, I finally
found things falling into place like a giant jigsaw puzzle.
It started to come together as though it was made to fit,
just-so. The words, recipes and photos. I felt quietly excited
every time I sat at my desk to add one more piece to the
puzzle. The result of all that puzzling is the book you now
hold in your hands. I don't quite know how to describe
it – I haven't figured that piece of the puzzle out yet! It's
a cross between a cookbook, a journal, a conversation, and
reflections on the world around me. I see it being as much
a bedside book just to read, as a cookbook, although I'd love
to think that the pages become splotched and smudged
from constant use.

Belinda ♥

# JANUARY

Tomato, herb and goat's cheese tart in no-roll cheese pastry

Eggplant with red wine vinegar, chilli and feta

One-pan chicken with marjoram, smoked paprika,
potatoes and tahini yoghurt

Audrey's Basque cheesecake

# Tomato, herb and goat's cheese tart in no-roll cheese pastry

My herb garden is in its full summer glory at the moment. It's absolutely chock-full of vivid-green mint and chives; spiky French tarragon with its impossibly aromatic, anise-scented leaves; great clumps of flat-leaf parsley; and tall spires of basil waving in the breeze. I've been having a field day with them – tossing them willy-nilly into just about everything I cook. The fridge and freezer are full of jars of fragrant green pesto and tubs of herb-scented soups. We've been eating bucket-loads of pasta tossed with extra-virgin olive oil, garlic, chilli, parmesan and handfuls of whatever herbs we pick. Brilliant-green zucchini and basil risotto has been featuring heavily on the menu and, as I'm a pastry cook at heart, I've been making all sorts of herb-laden tarts, including this lovely tomato one. It's very simple. Its beauty and freshness lie in using the most flavourful tomatoes you can lay your hands on, as well as plenty of chives, tarragon and basil in the herb mix, and a delicate, soft goat's cheese.

By all means, use ready-made pastry if you would like. However, at some stage, do give this cheese pastry a try. It takes no time to whiz up in a food processor and then only needs to be pressed into the tin and it's ready to go. It tastes wonderful – very cheesy and crunchy.

I hope your day is a gentle one.

Happy Sunday. Belinda 💜

*The fridge and freezer are full of jars of fragrant green pesto, tubs of herb-scented soups and, as I'm a pastry cook at heart, I've been making all sorts of herb-laden tarts.*

## Tomato, herb and goat's cheese tart in no-roll cheese pastry

SERVES 6

1 tablespoon extra-virgin
  olive oil
2 large brown onions,
  finely sliced
3 teaspoons brown sugar
2 teaspoons balsamic vinegar
3 cloves black garlic*, optional
4 large-ish (about 600g)
  just-ripe, flavourful
  tomatoes
4 × 60g eggs
¾ cup (180ml) milk
130ml pure cream (or crème
  fraîche)
1 heaped teaspoon sea salt
  flakes
freshly ground black pepper
¼ cup packed chopped herbs
  (ideally include French
  tarragon, basil and chives),
  or more to taste
120g soft goat's cheese
  or marinated feta
small herb leaves, optional,
  to garnish

**NO-ROLL CHEESE PASTRY**
1½ cups (225g) plain flour
100g tasty cheese, grated
120g cold unsalted butter,
  cubed
1 egg yolk (from 60g egg)
  mixed with 1 teaspoon
  water, to glaze

I've used large tomatoes for my tart, but cherry tomatoes are fine, too – they're just a little fiddlier to seed.

For the no-roll cheese pastry, put the flour and cheese into a food processor and quickly pulse together until they're well mixed. Add the butter and whiz everything together until the mixture looks like fine breadcrumbs. With the motor running, pour in 2 tablespoons (40ml) of iced water, and whiz until the mixture forms a ball around the blade.

Turn the pastry out onto a board (break off a 5 cent-size piece and pop it in the fridge, this can be used later to patch any cracks), then shape into a disc. Sit the disc in a 25cm–26cm loose-based tart tin and press it evenly over the base and sides, pushing up a little higher than the top of the tin. Take your time to do this, so you get a nice, even coverage. If the sides are too thin, they may crumble as the pastry cooks. Roll a tumbler over the base to help smooth out any bumps. If you like, you can crimp the top with your fingers to form a scalloped edge. Sit the tin on a baking sheet and pop it in the fridge to chill for at least 45 minutes. You can do this up to a day ahead of time, if you like.

Preheat your oven to 200°C. To blind bake the pastry, crush 2 large sheets of baking paper with your hands and open them out again (this softens the paper, making it easier to fit it into the tin). Completely cover the pastry with the sheets of paper, pressing them gently down into the corners. Spread baking weights, uncooked rice or dried beans all over the paper to about 1cm-deep.

Slide the baking tray into the oven and bake the tart shell for 25 minutes or until it's nearly set, lightly coloured and feels firm and dry. Remove from the oven and carefully lift out the sheets of baking paper with the baking weights. Don't worry if there are fine cracks in the pastry shell, just patch them with the reserved pastry.

Brush the egg yolk mixture all over the pastry, making sure it's well coated, then return the tart shell to the oven for 1–2 minutes, so the egg wash sets to a shiny glaze (this helps seal the pastry and stops the base becoming soggy once it's filled). When it's set, remove the tart shell from the oven and leave to cool in the tin on a wire rack.

For the filling, heat the oil in a medium frying pan over low–medium heat. Add the onion and cook, stirring regularly, for about 25 minutes or until it's meltingly soft. Sprinkle over the brown sugar and vinegar and continue cooking the onion, stirring frequently to make sure it doesn't stick to the pan, for another 3–4 minutes or until it becomes a lovely glossy, pale toffee colour. Remove the pan from the heat. Squeeze the black garlic from its skin and add it to

the onion mixture. Use the back of your spoon to mash it up and thoroughly mix it through. Set the pan aside to allow the mixture to cool.

Preheat your oven to 180°C. Halve the tomatoes and scoop out and discard the seeds (if you squeeze the halves quite hard, cut-side down over a bowl, most of the seeds will pop out). Put the halves to drain, cut-side down, on paper towel for 10 minutes or so, then slice into chunks or rounds. Sit these in a colander over a bowl until you're ready (you want as much liquid as possible to drain from the tomatoes or they'll make the base soggy). In a bowl, whisk the eggs to break them up, then whisk in the milk, cream (or crème fraîche), and salt and pepper. Finally, mix in the herbs. Pour the mixture into a jug, cover it lightly and place in the fridge until you're ready. You can do this a few hours ahead of time.

Once the onion mixture is cool, spread it over the base of the tart shell. Scatter the tomato evenly on top, then crumble over the goat's cheese or feta. Pull your oven shelf out halfway and transfer the tart (still on its tray) onto the shelf. Give the egg mixture a quick whisk as it will have settled, then drizzle it evenly into the shell. Gently slide the tart fully into the oven.

Bake for about 40 minutes or until the filling is still a little wobbly but set. The best way to test this is to pull the shelf out a little, then ever-so-lightly place your hand on the middle of the tart and give it a gentle jiggle. Remove the tart from the oven, leave it to settle in the tin for 5 minutes or so, then slide it onto a serving platter. Serve it warm or at room temperature scattered with a few small herb leaves.

**A NOTE ABOUT BUTTER**

I'm a bit of a butter fiend, I have to admit. Olive oil is wonderful, and I use it all the time, but nothing beats the flavour of good butter. And when I say good, I mean a butter that you enjoy. In the case of the recipes here, I use cultured unsalted butter – also called continental butter – which is basically made with a culture that gives the butter a delicate, clean flavour. There are some scrumptious imported butters like this, but they're usually costly, making them expensive to cook with. However, lots of supermarkets stock locally made cultured butter, which is terrific and is what I use. If you can't find it, you can use regular unsalted butter.

* Basically, black garlic is regular garlic that is heated over a long period of time (a little like fermenting), so that the sugars in it caramelise and darken. When you slice across the cloves, they look a bit like black jelly inside and have a wonderful rounded garlic flavour.

# Eggplant with red wine vinegar, chilli and feta

We've woken to a light sprinkle of rain, which I'm somewhat ashamed to admit, is the only the encouragement I needed to put off my walk this morning and, instead, curl up on the sofa with a cup of tea. There's something so soothing about watching the steam ribbon out of my cup, seeing the gentle greens in a garden grateful for rain, and observing the antics of our early morning visitors on the deck. At this stage, two very bossy peewits are strutting up and down as if they own the joint (which I'm pretty sure they think they do) and a baby rosella is trying to attract its mum's attention. Mum, in return, is studiously ignoring it, so there's a bit of a Mexican stand-off happening!

As often occurs at this time of year, my head fills with all sorts of recipe and food ideas. The notebook I keep on my desk to jot down these thoughts is already covered with scrawled notations and prompts to remind me of ideas I've had. Clive laughs at me when I return from my walks because my walking time is usually a creative time and I often arrive at the door, gesturing to him that I have a thought I don't want to lose, and rush into the office to put something down on paper before I forget. I wish inspiration would strike at home when it's much easier to do this!

*As often occurs at this time of year, my head fills with all sorts of recipe and food ideas.*

Yesterday, it was eggplant that caught my attention, as they're so beautiful at the moment. I jotted down a few notes on how I wanted to use them – cut into wedges, tossed in plenty of good olive oil and roasted in a hot oven (220°C) until deep-golden, then drizzled with a little red wine vinegar, sprinkled with very finely chopped chilli, and dolloped with scoops of luscious, chilli-infused feta made locally by our wonderful cheesemaker, Debra Allard (Deb's feta is really delicate and spoon-able, if there is such a word?). Later in the day when it finally came into being, we ate it on slices of chargrilled sourdough bread rubbed with a cut clove of garlic, trickled with extra-virgin olive oil and topped with the feta. I finished off with a handful of purslane leaves, a gift from my lovely neighbour. However, basil or mint would be very good, too. It was so easy, and I have to say, so delicious. I'd love to think that you might give it a try.

Happy Sunday. Belinda ♥

# One-pan chicken with marjoram, smoked paprika, potatoes and tahini yoghurt

I've been gently easing myself back into work mode as I look to the year ahead and what's coming up. I'm cutting back a little on teaching (not too much, I hasten to add, but just a few less classes throughout the year), and hopefully this will give me more opportunity to do some writing, experimenting with recipes, and to work in my garden. These past weeks I've realised, yet again, how important the latter is to me, actually to us. How good it is for our spirits and how much we miss it when we can't be out in it. With the somewhat cooler week we've had, and the wonderful soaking rain, we've finally been able to spend time outdoors again and it has been such a joy. Although I must say, it's looking rather sad and sorry, and we've lost quite a few plants from the heat and drought. Even so, it's been lovely to pick a few spinach leaves, a handful of chillies, a bunch of herbs, a couple of spring onions, and a lemon or two to use in salad dressings – or for our rather essential post-gardening, post-shower G&T!

The other part of the week has been spent in the kitchen working on recipes for my upcoming classes. As well as a few old favourites, I always try to have a range of new recipes as well. This is a little peek at what I'm working on at the moment – and what our friends are having for dinner this weekend, as it's wonderful to get their feedback. Thank goodness they don't seem to mind being guinea pigs!

This lovely chicken dish is a hands-down certainty for the class menu. It's based on a recipe in Darina Allen's gem of a book, *One Pot Feeds All*. The chicken, potatoes and garlic are lip-smackingly good – slightly crusty with a deep smoky flavour from the paprika. As you eat it, squeeze the gooey roasted garlic cloves from their skins onto your plate and scoop up a smidgen with each mouthful of chicken – it's so delicious!

Happy Sunday. Belinda

*Squeeze the gooey roasted garlic cloves from their skins onto your plate and scoop up a little bit with each mouthful of chicken – it's so delicious!*

# One-pan chicken with marjoram, smoked paprika, potatoes and tahini yoghurt

SERVES 6

700g Dutch cream (or other waxy) potatoes, peeled
1 medium-size brown onion, sliced into 8–10 wedges
8 skin-on chicken thigh cutlets
3 bay leaves
2 packed tablespoons finely chopped fresh marjoram (or oregano)
16 fat cloves garlic, unpeeled
2 finely chopped chillies, optional
⅓ cup (80ml) extra-virgin olive oil
¼ cup (60ml) lemon juice
1½ tablespoons smoked paprika
2 teaspoons sea salt flakes
freshly ground black pepper
bay leaves (or marjoram or oregano leaves), to garnish

## TAHINI YOGHURT

1 cup (280g) thick Greek-style yoghurt
1 dessertspoon tahini
1 small clove garlic, very finely chopped, or more to taste
¾ teaspoon sea salt flakes, or more to taste
50ml extra-virgin olive oil, plus a little extra, to garnish
freshly ground black pepper
1 bay leaf, to garnish, optional

Dutch cream potatoes are lovely for this recipe, as they hold their shape as they cook. But any other waxy potato will work well, too.

Preheat your oven to 230°C. Line a large, shallow-rimmed baking tray with baking paper. The size of the baking tray is important for this, as you want the mixture to fit comfortably. If the tray is too small, the chicken and potato won't brown as they should and will stew rather than roast. If you're at all concerned, err on the side of caution and divide the mixture evenly between 2 baking trays.

Cut the potatoes into fat wedges (you'll get 6 wedges out of a medium-size potato). Tumble them into a large bowl, add the onion wedges, chicken, bay leaves and marjoram or oregano. Prick each clove of garlic with a fine skewer and add them to the bowl (doing this will stop them exploding in the oven). Scrape in the chopped chilli, if using. Trickle over the olive oil and add the lemon juice, smoked paprika, and salt and pepper to taste. Use clean hands (or don a pair of prep gloves) to thoroughly mix everything together. Spread the mixture in a single layer in the baking tray or trays, sitting the chicken skin-side up and making sure it's not crowded.

Roast for 20 minutes, then reduce the heat to 180°C and roast for another 30–35 minutes or until the chicken skin is bronzed and the potato is golden with crisp edges.

While the chicken is cooking, make the tahini yoghurt. Put the yoghurt, tahini, garlic and salt into a bowl and mix together. Drizzle in the olive oil, whisking all the while, until the mixture is homogenised. Taste the mixture and add more salt, if needed. Scrape into a serving bowl, cover lightly and set aside in a cool spot until ready to use. Garnish with a soupçon of oil, pepper and a bay leaf (if using) just before serving.

Remove the baking tray from the oven and transfer everything, including any pan juices, to a large serving platter. Garnish with the bay leaves and serve with the tahini yoghurt.

*Sunday 26<sup>th</sup> January*

# Audrey's Basque cheesecake

For me, one of the great joys of holding my cooking classes locally is using produce and products that are grown or made a few kilometres from home. Even after many years of living here, I still pinch myself that we're able to cook with and eat such beautiful, nourishing food. Over the years, many of the producers have become friends and we feel very fortunate to know them. They're good, kind, hardworking and clever farmers, bakers, smallgoods artisans and cheesemakers.

I always start my classes by talking through the menu we're about to cook. I feel very proud when I'm able to explain that much of what we're using comes from friends. No one grows organic veggies quite like our dear friend, Palisa Anderson; or exotic fruits like those most green-fingered of growers, John and Lyndall Picone; or creates the magnificent bouquets of chillies, gingers and all sorts of greens that Kenrick Riley does and which we use in our curry bases. Then there are the makers, and one in particular, whose beautiful cheeses and dairy goods, made literally up the road from the cooking school, grace our table. Debra (the cheesemaker) and Jim (the farmer) Allard have their own small Jersey dairy herd and make everything from the girls' rich milk. Many of the cheeses appear on our cheeseboard, but even better, Debra's luscious crème fraîche, buttermilk, quark, ricotta, and kefir are all used in the food we cook.

There's one particular dish we make that brings many of these beautiful products together – it's a remarkable cheesecake, that was first introduced to me by the Allards' daughter, Audrey, who is a super-talented young pastry chef. It's based on a Basque cheesecake and it really is a winner. It's impossibly light and delicate, and not nearly as rich as you might imagine. Like all Basque cheesecakes it has a very dark, bittersweet surface, which is the perfect contrast to the gently creamy filling. It's delicious served with slightly sharp, roasted or poached fruits such as rhubarb, plums, apricots or tamarillos.

Happy Sunday. Belinda 💜

*Many of the producers have become friends and we feel very fortunate to know them. Good, kind, hardworking and clever farmers, bakers, smallgoods artisans and cheesemakers.*

# Audrey's Basque cheesecake

SERVES 12–16

500g quark (or cream cheese)
500g cottage cheese
(or ricotta)
350g caster sugar
finely grated zest of 2 lemons
1½ teaspoons vanilla extract
7 × 60g eggs, lightly beaten
¼ cup (35g) plain flour
(or gluten-free cornflour)
2 cups (500ml) crème fraîche
icing sugar, for dusting,
optional

Preheat your oven to 220°C. Butter a 25cm springform cake tin and line the base and sides with lightly buttered baking paper. Make sure the baking paper comes up about 3cm higher than the top of the tin, as the cheesecake will rise to quite a height as it bakes.

Put the quark (or cream cheese), cottage cheese (or ricotta) and caster sugar into a large food processor fitted with the steel blade and whiz, scraping down the sides occasionally, until the mixture is smooth. If your food processor is small, do this in batches. Whisk the lemon zest and vanilla extract into the eggs, then with the motor running, slowly pour in the egg mixture and whiz until creamy. You may need to stop and scrape down the sides once or twice as you go. Sprinkle in the flour (or cornflour) and pulse until combined. Scrape in the crème fraîche and pulse until well combined and smooth.

Pour the mixture into the prepared tin then pop in the oven. Bake the cheesecake for about 40 minutes or until it's puffed and very dark on top and the middle feels slightly wobbly, but firm. The best way to test this is to lightly place your hand on the middle of the tart and give it a gentle jiggle.

Carefully remove the cheesecake from the oven and sit it on a wire rack to cool completely in the tin. It will collapse quite a bit as it cools and the top may sink and crack a little.

It's rather lovely served barely warm or at room temperature, but is fragile to slice. To serve, release the sides of the cake tin and remove the baking paper from the sides. Wiggle and slide the cheesecake onto your serving platter, then gently wriggle the paper out from underneath (a long palette knife to lift the cake a little might help at this stage). Some liquid may weep from the cheesecake; if it does, just use paper towel to absorb it. Dust very lightly with icing sugar, if you like, although I must admit, I rather love the burnt, brown top.

The cake keeps exceptionally well in a sealed container in the fridge for up to 1 week, but do return it to room temperature before serving for the best flavour.

# FEBRUARY

Fragrant plum and apple jam

Super simple roasted tomato sauce

Roasted pineapple with hazelnut crumble and cardamom yoghurt cream

Lel's Hainan chicken rice

*Sunday 2ⁿᵈ February*

# Fragrant plum and apple jam

Why is it often the case that when we're at our busiest, we decide to add another layer of activity to what we're already doing? I've been on a tight deadline this week, not only climbing up and down ladders as we get our house ready to paint, but also putting the recipes together for my class and afternoon tea at the wonderful The Agrarian Kitchen Cooking School in Tasmania next weekend. So, of course, yesterday right in the middle of all this activity, I decided I just had to make plum jam from the beautiful plums I'd bought at the farmers market...as you do!

If you've never made jam before, plum jam is one of the easiest and most delectable of jams to get you started. The reason being that plums have high pectin and acid levels, so you're pretty much guaranteed a lovely jammy set (to ensure this, I also add a few apples to the pan as they're full of pectin, too). Depending on the variety of plums, the colour of the jam will vary from glowing rosy-pink to a deep, rich crimson when made with blood plums – all are utterly delicious.

*Why is it often the case that when we're at our busiest, we decide to add another layer of activity to what we're already doing?*

These jars are for my class goodie bags, but there's also extra to give to friends and, of course, some for us, to be dolloped into a mid-winter crostata, swirled through almond butter cake, eaten on hot, buttered toast (actually, I prefer cold toast, which I know is a bit unusual), and, best of all to me, plopped onto warm scones for a taste of summer sunshine on a chilly afternoon. The taste is difficult to describe – warm, mellow, fragrant, musky – it sounds a bit like a wine label, doesn't it?

I know the recipe looks a bit long-winded, but I promise it's easy. I was just trying to include as much information as possible to help you feel confident when you make it.

I'm off for a cup of tea and plum jam on cold toast!

Happy Sunday. Belinda ♥

# Fragrant plum and apple jam

MAKES APPROXIMATELY
14 × 150ML JARS

1.4kg just-ripe plums, washed
    well and dried
2 large (about 400g) Granny
    Smith apples, peeled
juice of 1 large lemon, pips
    reserved
1.5–1.6kg white sugar

Just a couple of things to note before you start; you can halve the recipe, if you like, which will help if you only have a smallish pan. You can also reduce the quantity of sugar somewhat, but as sugar helps with setting and preserving jam, the finished product may be a little runny, and it will need to be stored in the fridge or it will ferment and go mouldy. And, lastly, if there are any damaged or bruised patches on the plums, cut them out or the jam may become mouldy.

Slice the plums in half, then twist the halves in opposite directions to remove the stone. If the stones cling to the flesh, use a pointed paring knife to wiggle them free. Slice each half into 2, or if the plums are small, leave them in halves. Tumble them into a preserving pan, very large saucepan or stockpot (the juices will bubble up once the jam starts to thicken, so you need a large pan to stop them overflowing). Keep half a dozen of the stones, crack them with a nutcracker to remove the almond-like kernels inside and add these to the pan.

Slice the apples into 2cm pieces and add them to the pan along with the lemon juice. Chop the apple cores into 3–4 pieces and sit them in the centre of a square of muslin or cheesecloth along with the reserved lemon pips, then wrap the muslin around to form a little swag. Tie it tightly with string and tuck it down into the plum mixture.

Pour in 1 cup (250ml) cold water, then sit the pan over high heat. Bring the mixture to the boil, then reduce the heat to low so it bubbles gently – a lot of juices will flow out of the plums. Cook until the plum and apple are tender. The timing will vary for this, depending on the variety and ripeness of your plums. It may take anywhere from 20–35 minutes. The best way to see if they're ready is to crush them against the side of the pan with the back of your spoon.

Remove the pan from the heat. Scoop out the muslin swag and sit it in a small bowl. Hold the bowl over the pan and use the back of the spoon to press the swag against the bowl to extract as much liquid as possible, then tip the liquid into the pan. The pips and cores are full of the precious pectin you need to set the jam, so try to extract every last drop. Discard the swag.

Carefully, as the mixture will splash a lot, measure out the amount of hot plum mixture you have into a heatproof measuring jug, then just as carefully return it to the pan. Add an equal quantity of sugar and sit the pan back over high heat. Stir until the sugar dissolves. Now, clip a sugar thermometer to the side of the pan (this isn't essential, so don't worry if you don't have one, but it can help).

## STERILISING JARS

This recipe begs the question of how to sterilise jars, but just before I go into that, it's important to remember that the jars must be hot when you fill them with the hot jam, otherwise they may crack. So, you need to get your timing somewhat in sync with the jam when you sterilise the jars. There are a few ways to do this, but the two I mainly use are as follows:

• Wash the jars in warm, soapy water, rinse them thoroughly then sit them and their lids (as long as the lids aren't plastic or won't melt) on a baking tray. Put the tray with the jars into a cold oven then turn the heat to 130°C. Leave the jars for 30 minutes before carefully taking them out and covering them with a sheet of baking paper until you're ready to use them. Alternatively, if the jam isn't quite ready, you can just switch off the oven and leave the jars inside to keep hot.

• The other way, if you have a dishwasher, is to put the jars and their lids through the hottest cycle and leave them in once the cycle has finished, so they stay hot until you fill them.

Increase the heat to high and let the jam boil rapidly, stirring occasionally to make sure it isn't catching on the bottom, until it has reached setting point. I'll explain this in a moment, but before I do, it's important to be mindful that when jam is close to setting point it may bubble up rather alarmingly in the pan, so you need to keep an eye on it and adjust the temperature to ensure it doesn't boil over. It's hard to give a cooking time for this, as much depends on the size and shape of your pan. The larger and wider the pan, the better, as this allows for faster evaporation and quicker cooking, which preserves the fresh flavour of the plums. As a guide, a full batch in my large preserving pan takes about 25 minutes, but in a deeper pan, it would take longer.

Back to the setting point; there are a few ways to check this. First, if you're using a sugar thermometer, check the temperature has reached 105°C. The next thing to do is to dip a wooden spoon into the boiling jam, then lift it up high above the pan and let the jam drip back in. What you're hoping to see is those last few drops looking quite thick and syrupy and, ideally, running together and joining up – falling as more of a 'sheet' than individual drops (long fine tails on the jam drops will also do nicely). You can also spoon some jam onto an ice-cold saucer and put it in the freezer for a couple of minutes, then push your finger through it. If the surface wrinkles up a little and it leaves a clear trail, it's ready. Test the jam every minute or so and when it's ready, remove from the heat and let it settle for 10 minutes. Gently skim any pinkish froth from the surface with a metal spoon. A metal spoon is best as its sharp edge helps do this.

Stir the jam to distribute the fruit evenly then ladle it into hot and dry sterilised glass jars (see note, left), cover with a sheet of baking paper to protect them and leave to cool completely. When they're ready, remove the paper and seal the jars tightly. Wipe away any juices, label and date the jars and store in a cool, dark and dry place for 6–8 months.

# Super simple roasted tomato sauce

I can't begin to tell you just how fragrant the beautiful little tomatoes in this photograph were. As we leant over to shoot them, I was assailed by the sweet, earthy scent of perfectly ripe tomato. As soon as we'd taken the photos, I sliced half a dozen more, sprinkled them with salt, and we ate them on slices of thickly buttered sourdough bread – it was heaven!

What I was making from them is the simplest tomato pasta sauce ever. It's something that's on repeat at our table at the moment, as the weather is so muggy it's the easiest thing I can think of to cook.

To make it, all you need is about 1kg of halved, ripe cherry tomatoes, 3–4 whole cloves of garlic pricked with a fine skewer to stop them exploding in the oven (believe me, they do), and lots of extra-virgin olive oil – at least ½ cup (125ml). A few chillies are optional, but essential if you're a chilli lover like me. Mix the tomatoes, garlic, olive oil, and chillies, if using, in a big bowl, then tumble them out onto a large baking tray lined with baking paper. Arrange the tomatoes, cut-side up, then sprinkle with a few pinches of sugar and salt. Put the tray into a preheated 180°C oven for about 35 minutes or until the tomatoes are squishy and smell wonderful. I then get out my trusty mouli and run the whole lot through it (my lovely friend and clever cooking teacher, Paola Bacchia, tells me Italians call a mouli, a 'passatutto', which sounds so much more lyrical to me). It's one of my favourite kitchen utensils, and definitely worthy of a post of its own. The mouli separates the skins and seeds, while crushing the meltingly soft tomatoes and garlic into a puree. That's all there is to it! Taste the sauce to see if it needs a bit more salt, a dash of balsamic vinegar, or a handful of basil leaves and some sliced Kalamata olives, then tip the lot over cooked pasta. It's so good! Many times recently this easy-peasy sauce has been an absolute saviour for me when the day has flashed by and I have no idea what we're going to have for dinner. I hope it might help you, too.

Happy Sunday. Belinda 🖤

*My lovely friend, Paola, tells me Italians call a mouli, a 'passatutto', which sounds so much more lyrical to me than mouli.*

**P.S.** If you don't have a mouli, you can whiz everything in a blender, but you may want to sieve out the skins and seeds.

**P.P.S.** The basic sauce, without the basil and olives, freezes really well, too. It will keep for a couple of months in the freezer.

# Roasted pineapple with hazelnut crumble and cardamom yoghurt cream

And so, the testing goes on. I've been working on menus for my cooking classes and thus far have only managed to totally confuse myself. Every time I feel I have the menu 'just so' I think of something else that might work even better. I have a bit of a love-and-hate relationship with this process – it's exciting working out the menu, but I just wish I knew when to stop! Still, having scoured the farmers market on Friday to see what produce is at its best, at least I have the bones of what we're going to cook sorted. Many of the greens are sad after our constant rain and heat, but there are little pockets of joy – vivid red peppers, tomatoes, all sorts of eggplant and sweetly fragrant pineapples. Add to these lipstick-pink dragon fruit and plump finger limes, and I feel as though I'm getting somewhere – thank goodness. Decisions, decisions. Still, shortly I'll put down my pen, and head off for a swim before an afternoon working in the garden, leaving it all to simmer in the background of my mind. Hopefully, as it does so, everything will start to gel.

Happy Sunday. Belinda ♥

**P.S.** A quick update: having swum and gardened, I'm relieved to say that I've decided on the dessert. We'll make pineapple roasted with brown sugar, orange juice and cardamom, topped with cardamom-scented yoghurt cream and a crunchy hazelnut crumble. Phew, one down and only six more recipes to go!

*There are little pockets of joy – vivid red peppers, tomatoes, all sorts of eggplant, sweetly fragrant pineapples, lipstick-pink dragon fruit and plump finger limes.*

# Roasted pineapple with hazelnut crumble and cardamom yoghurt cream

SERVES 4

1 medium-size (or 2 small)
  pineapples peeled,
  quartered lengthwise,
  and cored
⅓ cup (75g) packed brown
  sugar
⅓ cup (80ml) orange juice,
  or more if needed
seeds from 3 cardamom pods*

**HAZELNUT CRUMBLE**
100g whole hazelnuts
80g plain flour
50g brown sugar
¼ teaspoon salt
50g cold unsalted butter,
  cut into small pieces

**CARDAMOM YOGHURT CREAM**
200ml thickened cream
100ml thick Greek-style
  yoghurt
1 tablespoon brown sugar
¾ teaspoon vanilla extract
freshly ground seeds from
  5 cardamom pods*
  (or ½ teaspoon ground
  cardamom) or more to taste

Preheat your oven to 190°C and line a large baking tray with baking paper

For the hazelnut crumble, tumble the hazelnuts into a food processor fitted with the steel blade and pulse until they're fairly coarsely chopped (there will be both small and large pieces of nut). Tip them into a large bowl.

Now add the flour, sugar and salt to the processor and whiz together for 10 seconds. Add the butter and whiz again until the mixture resembles medium breadcrumbs. Add the mixture to the bowl of chopped hazelnuts and gently stir them together. Spread the mixture out evenly onto the prepared baking tray. Bake the crumble for 15–20 minutes, stirring occasionally, until it browns, smells lovely and is toasty and cooked through. Remove the tray from the oven and sit it on a wire rack. Leave the crumble to cool completely, then put it into an airtight container and seal tightly. If you're using the crumble within a day or two, store it at cool room temperature, otherwise, pop the container in the freezer and remove as much crumble as you need about 10 minutes before serving. What I love about this is that it keeps well in the freezer for up to 4 weeks, so you can sprinkle it on all sorts of fruit.

Reduce your oven temperature to 180°C. To roast the pineapple, sit the quarters in a medium-size gratin dish (or other ovenproof glass or ceramic dish), so they fit snugly. Put the brown sugar, orange juice and cardamom seeds into a bowl and whisk them together until the sugar dissolves. Drizzle this mixture evenly over the pineapple quarters, then turn them around so they're well coated. Pop the dish into the oven and roast for about 1¼ hours, turning the pineapple quarters every 20 minutes or so and basting them with the liquid in the base of the dish until they're a gorgeous, rich golden-brown colour. If you find the liquid starts to scorch and has nearly disappeared, just add a little more orange juice. When it is ready, remove the dish from the oven and set it aside to cool. The pineapple can be cooked a few hours prior to serving.

While the pineapple is roasting, make the cardamom yoghurt cream. Put the cream, yoghurt, brown sugar, vanilla and ground cardamom seeds into a medium-size bowl and stir them together. Cover the bowl and pop it in the fridge. Just prior to serving, lightly whip the mixture until it thickens and forms soft, creamy peaks.

To serve, slice the pineapple into bite-size pieces (hang onto any juices in the baking dish). Divide the pineapple evenly between 4 small dessert bowls or goblets and trickle any reserved juices over the top. Dollop a good spoonful of the cardamom yoghurt cream alongside, and sprinkle a little crumble over the top. Spoon any remaining cardamom cream into a bowl to serve separately. I usually put out a bowl of the leftover crumble, too, and I find it gets vacuumed up!

* Removing the dark seeds from cardamom pods can be a bit fiddly, but fortunately the seeds themselves are becoming more widely available, so do keep an eye out for them. I prefer to grind cardamom seeds for the freshest, most aromatic flavour but you can also use ready-ground cardamom.

*Sunday 23rd February*

# Lel's Hainan chicken rice

Endless possibilities... a gentle, rainy afternoon; a friend's treasured recipe; and, most wonderful of all, time to do whatever I wish. I spent yesterday afternoon happily pootling in my kitchen. Pootling can mean different things to each of us but, basically, it's a lovely word I learnt from my husband, which means nothing more than tinkering about doing something you enjoy without pressure or constraints of time.

I'd have to say, a lot of my pootling gets done in my kitchen. It's only small, but a lovely place to cook. One window looks out onto our veggie garden, which at the moment is a sea of lavender, green and gold spikes, as I've let the mustard, parsley and rocket go to seed, and the chives, which have suddenly shot up and flowered, are a mass of lavender pompoms. If I look the other way, I see the deck; yesterday, I couldn't help but burst out laughing as I watched our resident baby magpie (who has an injured claw) having a toe-to-toe (probably that should be, claw-to-claw) stand-off with the wonga pigeon over who is top bird – they really are hilarious!

A folder full of recipes I hope to try accompanied me into the kitchen and I took my time choosing what I'd make. I love this folder. It's a muddle of newspaper and magazine clippings, recipe ideas I've scrawled on scraps of paper, and, its most precious cargo of all, recipes I've been given by family and friends. They all wind up in this rather tattered, but much-loved binder waiting for their chance to shine. Yesterday, it was the turn of a favourite recipe, Hainan chicken rice, from a dear friend, Lel. I have to admit I fiddled with it a bit (I know, I know, I can't help myself!), but the essence of the recipe shone through, and as we ate, it conjured up memories of many happy meals spent around her table. It's by no means a classic version of this famous dish, but it is utterly delicious. It's the kind of comfort food that nourishes body and soul.

Happy Sunday. Belinda ♥

*Pootling can mean different things to each of us but, basically, it's a lovely word I learnt from my husband, which means nothing more than tinkering about doing something you enjoy without pressure or constraints of time.*

# Lel's Hainan chicken rice

SERVES 4

## CHICKEN

1 heaped tablespoon whole
   black peppercorns
4 large spring onions, cut into
   6cm lengths
1 large whole bunch of
   coriander (roots and all),
   well washed
4cm piece fresh ginger, sliced
   and bashed with the flat
   of a knife
1½ teaspoons sea salt flakes
1 × 1.6kg (or thereabouts)
   whole organic or free-range
   chicken, at cool room
   temperature
1½ tablespoons sea salt
   flakes or coarse salt, extra,
   for rubbing
2–3 teaspoons sesame oil
coriander leaves, to garnish
sliced cucumber, to serve,
   optional

## RICE

1½ tablespoons light olive oil
   or peanut oil
1 clove garlic, finely chopped
1 tablespoon finely chopped
   fresh ginger
1 large spring onion, very
   finely sliced
1½ cups (330g) jasmine rice
1 teaspoon sea salt flakes
1 pandan leaf, knotted,
   optional

For the chicken, pour 3½ litres of water into a large saucepan that will hold the chicken and water comfortably. Add the peppercorns, spring onion, bunch of coriander, ginger, and 1½ teaspoons sea salt to the water, then bring to the boil over high heat.

Meanwhile, briskly rub the chicken all over with the extra 1½ tablespoons sea salt flakes or coarse salt to thoroughly clean the skin, then rinse it under cool water.

Lower the chicken into the pan, breast-side down, and let the liquid return to the boil. Reduce the heat to low so that just a few bubbles rise steadily to the surface. Leave the chicken to cook, uncovered, for 40 minutes, skimming off any froth that floats to the top. You'll find that the chook tends to bob to the surface, so I sit a heatproof plate on top to ensure it stays submerged. Turn off the heat, cover the pan tightly and leave the chicken to steep in the liquid until you're ready to serve (the chicken will be fine like this for up to 1 hour). Sit a strainer over a heatproof measuring jug, then ladle 2¼ cups (560ml) of the chicken stock into the jug. Set this aside to cook the rice.

For the rice, warm the oil in a large, heavy-based saucepan over low heat. Add the garlic, ginger and spring onion, and cook, stirring occasionally, for 3 minutes or until soft and slightly translucent. Increase the heat to high, add the rice, salt, and pandan leaf, if using, and give it a good stir so the grains are coated in the oil mixture. Pour in the reserved 2¼ cups (560ml) chicken stock and bring to the boil. As soon as the stock is bubbling rapidly, reduce the heat to very low and leave the rice to cook, covered, for exactly 12 minutes. Now, turn off the heat and lay a folded tea towel between the lid and the saucepan, wedging the lid on firmly so no steam escapes. Leave the rice to sit like this for 10–20 minutes. When you're ready to serve, scoop it into a bowl.

## GINGER AND SPRING ONION

1 large or 2 smaller bunches
  spring onions, finely sliced
160g fresh ginger, peeled
  and finely chopped
1 teaspoon sea salt flakes
150ml light olive oil
  or peanut oil

## CHILLI SAUCE

2 small red chillies,
  finely chopped
½ cup (125ml) light soy sauce

While the rice is cooking, make the ginger and spring onion topping. Sprinkle about ⅕ of the spring onion and ⅕ of the ginger into a medium-size heatproof serving bowl, then sprinkle a little of the salt over the top. Repeat this layering until all the spring onion, ginger, and salt are used. Heat the oil in a small saucepan until it's smoking hot (this is crucial, as it needs to be very hot to soften and partially cook the spring onion mixture). Carefully pour the oil over the mixture. You will hear it sizzle and get a whoosh of wonderful fragrance. Set the mixture aside.

To make the chilli sauce, simply mix the chilli and soy sauce together, then pour the mixture into a small serving bowl. Set aside.

To serve the chicken, carefully remove the chicken from the saucepan, reserving the stock. Pat it dry and rub it with the sesame oil, then using a hefty knife or cleaver cut into pieces, Chinese-style (you will notice the bones are dark-pink inside). Alternatively, carve it as you would roast chicken, but divide it into smaller pieces (for example, separate the leg and thigh, and slice the breast fillets neatly across the grain into large pieces).

Transfer the chicken to a large, shallow bowl or serving platter and trickle a little of the chicken stock over the top, then scatter with coriander leaves. Serve with the rice, chilli sauce, spring onion and ginger mixture, and a little of the chicken broth. As these dishes are quite luscious, you might like to add a bowl of sliced cucumber for a fresh contrast.

Strain any leftover chicken stock and store it in the freezer for up to 3 months. It will have a gingery flavour and is perfect for cooking the next Hainan chicken you make; you'll only need to add water to make the quantity up to 3½ litres. Each batch becomes richer and more chicken-y and adds to the overall flavour of the dish.

**P.S.** If you'd like to eat the chicken cool, gently lift it out of the stock after the 40 minutes cooking time, being extra-careful not to tear the skin, and allow any liquid to drain from the cavity. The easiest way to do this is by inserting the handle of a wooden spoon through the cavity of the chicken so you can scoop it out of the pan without damaging the skin. Immediately plunge the chicken into a deep bowl (or saucepan, if you don't have a deep enough bowl) of iced water to completely submerge. Leave the chicken to cool in the water for 1 hour. Plunging into the iced water is what gives the chicken its silky texture and jellied breast meat. Reserve the chicken stock to serve alongside and to keep for the next time you make this dish.

# MARCH

Simple poached figs

Raspberry hand pies with rough puff pastry

Goat's cheese and herb omelette

My tried-and-true hummus

Smoked paprika and rosemary pide crisps

*Sunday 1ˢᵗ March*

# Simple poached figs

As I write this, it's the crack of dawn and I'm sitting outside with a cup of tea, revelling in the coolness and beauty of the world waking up. I've always loved the early morning, it has a stillness and quietness that inevitably makes me feel reflective and content, and to want for nothing more than to be where I am, as I am. I suppose in a way, this peaceful time is my meditation. Although, as the sun rises, I can already feel the tug of the garden drawing me in as I start to notice all the work that needs doing. But just for this little while, I resist, as I don't want to let these moments pass unnoticed. Soon it will be time for me to gently rouse the sleepyheads as we're off for a swim before it gets too hot, and I'd like to have some figs cooked before we leave. They're a Sunday breakfast treat for us and so easy to make. If you'd like to give them a try, all you need do is halve 8–10 fresh figs and sit them, cut-side up, in a ceramic oven dish. Drizzle them with a mixture of honey and melted butter, roughly ¼ cup (60ml) of each, the finely grated zest and juice from half a large orange, and a sprinkle of cinnamon. Pop the whole lot into a hot oven (200°C) for 15 minutes, let them cool a little, then eat them with a dollop of creamy, Greek-style yoghurt and a drizzle of honey, if you like. They're such a simple breakfast treat.

Happy Sunday. Belinda 🖤

*I've always loved the early morning, it has a stillness and quietness that inevitably makes me feel reflective and content, and to want for nothing more than to be where I am, as I am.*

*Sunday 8th March*

# Raspberry hand pies with rough puff pastry

We're in the throes of gearing up for our first classes of the cooking school year (we don't start until March as it's just too hot for cooking during summer here). Benches have been scrubbed to within an inch of their life, walls washed, ovens tested, vases and buckets are lined up waiting to be filled with armfuls of flowers and foliage raided not only from our own garden, but those of kind friends, too. Baskets are ready for their cargo of fruit, veggies and our beautiful rainbow eggs. And I must say, as I glanced over my shoulder before we shut the doors on our efforts, I couldn't help but smile as the kitchen positively sparkled. Back at home, a load of aprons and napkins are waiting to be ironed, and I'm about to launch into making a big batch of fragrant plum and apple jam (see recipe, page 28) to go into our goodie bags. So yes, still lots to do, but it's exciting!

*Vases and buckets are lined up waiting to be filled with armfuls of flowers and foliage raided not only from our own garden, but those of kind friends, too.*

Our first classes next weekend are on the whys and wherefores of pastry-making, so in amongst the to-ing and fro-ing to get set-up, I've been working on some new pastry recipes. These rather rustic hand pies made with the lightest, most gloriously crunchy pastry have had the seal of approval from my number-one taste-tester who also happens to be a puff pastry fiend. The filling is a simple compote of lightly sweetened, late-season raspberries – those beautiful, dark-crimson ones that are so intensely flavoured. Its tang is just the right contrast to the buttery pastry, especially with a spoonful of softly whipped crème fraîche or cream on the side. Then again, in my book, most things are better for a dollop of cream!

Happy Sunday. Belinda 🖤

# Raspberry hand pies with rough puff pastry

MAKES 12–14

1 eggwhite (from 60g egg),
   lightly beaten
1 tablespoon sugar (white,
   Demerara or raw), optional
icing sugar, for dusting
softly whipped crème fraîche,
   cream or vanilla ice-cream,
   to serve, optional

**ROUGH PUFF PASTRY**

250g plain flour, plus extra,
   for dusting
1 teaspoon salt
250g chilled (but not ice-cold)
   unsalted butter, cut into
   2cm pieces

**RASPBERRY FILLING**

200g fresh (or frozen)
   raspberries
⅓ cup (75g) caster sugar
20g cornflour

These gorgeous little pies are hugely popular in our classes and regularly appear on our menu for morning tea. The pastry, a wonderfully crisp and flaky rough puff pastry, is a recipe I often demonstrate to our students as it really is remarkably easy to make and utterly delicious.

To make the rough puff pastry, put the flour and salt into the bowl of a food processor fitted with the steel blade and whiz them together for 15 seconds. Add the butter and pulse briefly until the butter is in 1cm pieces. Tip the mixture into a medium-size bowl, then slowly drizzle in ½ cup (125ml) iced water in concentric circles over the top, mixing with your hand as you go so the pastry forms a crumbly mass. You don't want to knead it, but rather just bring it together using a circular gathering motion.

Lightly dust your benchtop with flour and tip the pastry onto it. Don't worry that it barely holds together and looks quite shaggy with damp and dry patches – that's exactly how it's meant to be. Use a pastry scraper to help shape it into a rough 15cm × 10cm rectangle, with a narrow end facing you. Flour your rolling pin and roll the dough away from you until it's roughly 3 times as long as it is wide. Use your scraper to fold it into thirds and shape into as neat a rectangle as possible (try to keep the pastry in shape with sharp corners and neat edges). Turn the dough 90 degrees clockwise, so an open end is facing you, and repeat this rolling and folding twice, always neatening the dough into a rectangle between each turn. If you find the pastry is sticking to your benchtop, gently lift it with the scraper and dust a little more flour underneath. The idea with both puff and rough puff pastry is to laminate the butter between thin sheets of pastry, so as the butter melts and gives off steam, the pastry rises. If you find that the pastry becomes quite soft as you roll and the butter is being absorbed (you should see streaks of butter through it), return it to the fridge for 20 minutes or so before continuing the rolling and turning process.

Wrap the pastry in baking paper then foil and chill for at least 30 minutes before using. The pastry can be used now, or if you would like more layers, you can roll, turn and rest it again. The pastry keeps for up to 2 days in the fridge or 3 months in the freezer.

To make the raspberry filling, put the raspberries and sugar into a medium-size saucepan and gently mix them together. Leave them to sit for 30 minutes to help the raspberries release their juices.

Stir in the cornflour, then sit the pan over medium heat and bring the mixture to the boil, stirring regularly. Allow it to bubble for 40 seconds or so, until it has thickened, scraping the bottom of the pan occasionally with your spoon to stop it catching. Remove the pan from the heat and scrape the mixture into a heatproof bowl. Allow it to cool without stirring. If you stir the filling at this stage, you run the risk of the cornflour breaking down and thinning out. The filling can be used as soon as it's cool, or can be kept in the fridge in a sealed container for 2–3 days.

Line 1–2 baking trays with baking paper. To make the pies, roll out the pastry on a lightly floured surface until it's about 3–4mm thick. Use a small bowl or cardboard template about 11cm in diameter to cut out as many rounds of pastry as you can. Remove the pastry scraps and set them aside.

Brush the circumference of the pastry rounds with a little eggwhite. Scoop a smallish spoonful (just less than a tablespoon) of the raspberry mixture into the middle of the rounds, then quickly lift up one side of the pastry and press it onto the other side, enclosing the filling so you end up with a half-moon shape. Use a fork to decoratively squish the edges together, then make 3 × 1cm cuts in the top of the pies to form air vents so steam can escape. Sit the pies on the prepared baking trays. Layer the pastry scraps on top of each other and roll them out, too. Once all the pies are made, chill them for at least 30 minutes. Reserve any leftover eggwhite.

Preheat your oven to 200°C. Remove the pies from the fridge and lightly brush the tops with reserved eggwhite, making sure it doesn't clog the steam vents. Sprinkle with a little sugar, then pop the trays in the oven.

Bake the pies for about 20 minutes or until the pastry is deep-golden and puffed. Let them settle on the tray for a couple of minutes, then transfer to a wire rack to cool. They're delicious eaten warm or at room temperature. Dust with icing sugar and serve with softly whipped crème fraîche or cream. (They're also inordinately delicious with vanilla ice-cream!). If you should have any pies left, they freeze well. Reheat from frozen in a 180°C oven for 15–20 minutes or until they've crisped up again.

*Sunday 15ᵗʰ March*

# Goat's cheese and herb omelette

What a difference a week makes! After days of steady, soaking rain, rather than crisp, brown grass and stressed trees that have shed their leaves, I'm now looking out my window onto the soft greens of new growth. It's beautiful. There's the drip and rush and run of water everywhere. These past few days, on my morning walk, there have been water birds splashing in once-dry creek beds and a right royal orchestra of frogs croaking for all their worth.

My veggie garden, too, seems to have sprung up overnight. Our basil that struggled through the relentless heat is suddenly lush and emerald green, and the zinnias (or 'Donald's' as I call them, after the dear friend who gave me the seeds, and which I plant in with the vegetables as I love their cheery faces) are standing tall and just starting to flower. There are loads of chillies and the few hardy spinach plants that have survived are sprouting new leaves. Although the garden looks quite bare, we've managed to pick a few things each day. The spinach was steamed then sautéed, providing an earthy-green base for poached eggs on toast; the chillies and spring onions went into stir-fries; and the chives and parsley flavoured the beautiful golden eggs that we use for our goat's cheese omelettes – my favourite quick meal.

Take 2–3 eggs, a small handful of chopped herbs, a sprinkle of salt, and some crumbled goat's cheese, along with a hot pan and less than 5 minutes of your time, and you have the perfect meal – especially served with a glass of wine. It's something we eat regularly and the first recipe I teach my nieces and nephews before they go out into the world. If you'd like to try it, using a fork, very lightly whisk together the eggs, herbs and salt. Heat a 24cm non-stick frying pan over high heat until it's hot. Add a small pat of butter and use a wad of paper towel to swish it around the pan. Tip in the egg mixture and cook, stirring constantly with the fork and tilting the pan to let any wet mixture run into the gaps. When it's still a bit wet on top, crumble over the goat's cheese, roll the omelette onto itself, then tip it out onto a warm plate – the whole cooking process should take less than 1 minute. And that's it, dinner in no time flat!

Happy Sunday. Belinda ♥

*It's something we eat regularly, and is the first recipe I teach my nieces and nephews before they go out into the world.*

# My tried-and-true hummus

I love these first few weeks of March. I'm not in full-on work mode yet, but find my days are a blend of early morning swims, spring cleaning (I know it's autumn, but I never did get to it in spring), doing all sorts of odd jobs in the garden that have been waiting patiently to be addressed, and my greatest pleasure of all – creating new recipes for my classes and books.

Without other pressing things to attend to, I feel incredibly fired up creatively to finetune recipes, come up with ideas, and just generally try out new things. As I made this hummus yesterday, I realised yet again that it's the simple dishes I love. I have no doubt there are zillions of recipes for hummus, but the real beauty of it lies in finding that wonderful balance of flavours, texture and temperature when everything is 'just right'. We ate this while it was still warm and almost cloud-like in its lightness – it was truly ambrosial. As I said, simple things, but when they're really good, they can be extraordinary.

*We ate this while it was still warm and almost cloud-like in its lightness – it was truly ambrosial.*

Happy Sunday. Belinda ♥

**P.S.** This and the pide crisp recipe that follows (page 56) are a made-in-heaven combination. Smoky, herby crisps meet earthy, fluffy hummus. What could be better?

# My tried-and-true hummus

MAKES 3–4 CUPS

¾ cup (170g) dried chickpeas
½ teaspoon bicarbonate
 of soda
3 cloves garlic, 2 crushed
 and 1 finely chopped
1 dried red chilli
1 bay leaf
½ cup (125ml) freshly
 squeezed lemon juice,
 or more to taste
2 teaspoons sea salt flakes,
 or more to taste
1 cup (250ml) tahini
⅓ cup (80ml) extra-virgin
 olive oil
1 slightly heaped teaspoon
 freshly ground cumin seeds
a little olive oil, a pinch of
 smoked paprika, finely sliced
 chilli and tiny herb leaves, to
 garnish, optional

**You'll find the flavours of the cumin and garlic will
become a bit more pronounced over a few days,
so keep this in mind when you make it.**

Wash the chickpeas really well and check them for any
little stones or discoloured peas. Put them to soak in a large
bowl of cold water. Sprinkle the bicarbonate of soda into
the water and stir to ensure it dissolves (the bicarbonate of
soda helps the chickpeas to soften more quickly). You need
about 4 times the amount of water as there are chickpeas.
Leave them in a cool spot overnight. If the weather is warm,
it's a good idea to pop them in the fridge, otherwise they can
ferment and start to bubble.

The next day, drain the chickpeas and rinse them again.
Put them into a large saucepan and cover with cold water by
at least an index finger-length. Add the crushed garlic cloves,
chilli and bay leaf to the pan. Bring the water to the boil, then
reduce the heat so it bubbles steadily. Cook the chickpeas
until they're tender and creamy but not mushy – if the
water level starts to look low, top it up with very hot water.
Spoon away any impurities that form on the surface as the
chickpeas cook. The cooking time can vary widely depending
on just how fresh the chickpeas are; recently dried chickpeas
can cook in about 45 minutes, but older ones may take up
to 1½ hours or more. The best way to check is to scoop out
a couple and try them – they should be tender. As soon as
they're ready, thoroughly drain the chickpeas but hang
onto about ⅔ cup (160ml) of the cooking water to thin the
hummus a little, if necessary. Pluck out and discard the garlic
cloves, chilli and bay leaf.

Scrape the chopped garlic into a blender or food processor
(a blender is ideal as it makes for a finer texture), then add
the lemon juice and salt. Leave them to sit for 5 minutes
– this helps soften the powerful bite of the garlic. Add the
tahini and ½ cup (125ml) iced water and puree until the
mixture is smooth. With the motor running, pour in the olive
oil in a fine stream. When the mixture is lovely and creamy,
stop the machine and add all but 1 tablespoon of chickpeas
and the ground cumin. Continue to blend everything
together until the mixture is as smooth, light and creamy
as possible. This may take 5–6 minutes, depending on your
blender or processor. If the hummus seems a bit too thick
and dense, pour in some of the reserved cooking water to
thin it a little (remember that it will thicken a bit more once
it cools). Finally, taste the hummus and add a little more
lemon juice, salt or cumin to balance out the flavours.

To serve, spoon the hummus into a bowl. Drizzle over a little olive oil and sprinkle with the reserved chickpeas, smoked paprika, sliced chilli and herb leaves, if using.

The hummus keeps well in a tightly covered container in the fridge for up to 1 week. Just remember to bring it to room temperature before serving.

*Sunday 29ᵗʰ March*

# Smoked paprika and rosemary pide crisps

I love bread, but I don't make 'proper' bread often. Soda breads and quick breads, yes, but we have so many wonderful bakers locally that I'm happy to leave the sourdoughs, ryes, wholegrains and Turkish breads in their far more skilful hands.

Speaking of Turkish bread, I have to confess that I have a particular weakness for it and feel quite alarmed when we don't have any tucked away in the freezer. I use it constantly for sandwiches, or torn into rough pieces and sautéed in olive oil to make crunchy little croutons for soups and salads and, best of all, left to stale a bit and made into these scrumptious pide crisps that are perfect to eat with a drink. They came about when one of my students whipped them up with bread leftover from a class (I love how my classes are a two-way street – I'm often given wonderful tips and recipe ideas by our lovely attendees). I jotted down a few notes to trigger my memory for later, and have since come up with this recipe, which I actually think should carry a warning as they're so addictive it's hard to stop at one!

Happy Sunday. Belinda ♥

*I actually think these should carry a warning as they're so addictive it's hard to stop at one!*

# Smoked paprika and rosemary pide crisps

MAKES 20-24

200ml extra-virgin olive oil,
    or more as needed
1 teaspoon smoked paprika
¾ teaspoon sea salt flakes
1 clove garlic, crushed
    (or finely chopped for
    a stronger flavour)
300g stale Turkish bread,
    cut into 8mm-thick slices
6 large rosemary sprigs
    (or oregano), finely chopped

Just a little note of caution as this recipe is deceptively simple: to make the crisps the most delicious they can be, you actually need to take care in every part of it, such as slicing the bread the right thickness, oiling it to the edges, and cooking for just the right amount of time to ensure the crisps are crunchy but not hard. Please don't be tempted to reduce the amount of oil as they won't taste nearly as delicious as they should. If your bread is too fresh and difficult to slice to the desired thickness, simply pop it in the freezer to firm up before slicing.

Preheat your oven to 175°C. Line 1 large or 2 small baking sheets with baking paper and set aside.

Thoroughly mix together the oil, smoked paprika, salt and garlic in a jug. Lay the bread slices on the prepared sheet or sheets. Give the oil mixture a really good stir, then brush the slices liberally with half the mixture, making sure you brush right to the edges of each slice. Scatter half the chopped rosemary evenly over the top.

Put the baking sheet in the oven and cook the slices for about 8 minutes. After this time, remove the sheet from the oven and carefully turn the slices with tongs. Brush over the remaining oil mixture evenly, especially dab it onto any dryish-looking patches – if you find you run low on the mixture, just add a splash more oil to whatever remains in the jug. Scatter the remaining rosemary over the top and return the sheet to the oven. Bake for another 5–8 minutes or until the crisps are golden and bubbling. You may find some slices colour and cook more rapidly than others; if this is the case, remove them as they're ready, otherwise they can become a bit too hard to bite into.

Put the baking sheet on a wire rack and let the slices cool and crisp. Store them in an airtight container, where they should keep well for at least 10 days. These are delicious just as is or as a scoop for dips, such as my tried-and-true hummus (see recipe, page 52).

# APRIL

Slow-cooked vanilla quinces

Quince and hazelnut tart

Dark chocolate and halvah semifreddo

Salted pistachio brittle

Gigantes plaki (Greek-style baked beans)

# Slow-cooked vanilla quinces and a quince and hazelnut tart

Much to my joy and despite our ongoing heat, the first quinces of the season appeared at Friday's farmer's market. There was only one basket, but as though drawn by a magnet, they were swooped upon by early bird quince aficionados and within minutes they were gone. I'm very glad to report that three made it into my shopping trolley along with persimmons (another fleeting autumn treat) and a paper bag full of chestnut mushrooms. Autumn really has arrived!

The mushrooms went into a pie for dinner last night, and we'll have to wait patiently for the persimmons to become squishy and sweet, but the quinces went straight into a big saucepan, along with sugar, vanilla and orange zest, and onto the cooktop.

Cooking is full of alchemy, but I think, perhaps, one of the most wondrous transformations of all is how with sugar and long, slow cooking, the hard, ivory flesh of these beautiful fruits is transformed to a dazzling rosy-pink and their flavour mellowed from raw tannic sharpness to an extraordinarily fragrant blend of pears, apples and so much more. It's nigh impossible to describe.

*There was only one basket, but as though drawn by a magnet, they were swooped upon by early bird quince aficionados and within minutes they were gone.*

Once cooked, I use them in many ways – for breakfast with a dollop of yoghurt or tucked into an apple or pear crumble (the fragrance from just a few slices permeates the whole dish and transforms this homely pudding into something truly wonderful). They're also divine baked into a simple pound cake, which only needs a dusting of icing sugar to be quite perfect, and in tarts like the beautiful one here, where they're nestled into a squidgy hazelnut frangipane filling.

Happy Sunday. Belinda ♥

## Slow-cooked vanilla quinces

SERVES 6–8

3 large (or 4 medium) quinces
juice of 1 lemon
2 cups (440g) white sugar
long spiral of lemon zest
long spiral of mandarin
    or orange zest
1 vanilla bean, split

I make batch after batch of these lovely quinces when they're in season and keep them in the fridge. You won't need the full quantity for the tart but as they keep so well, it's wonderful to have them on hand.

Give the quinces a really good scrub in cool water to remove any greyish fuzz from the skin, then pat them dry. Just a gentle reminder before you start peeling, quinces are *very* hard (similar to pumpkin to handle), so you need to be really careful when you're working with them.

Squeeze the juice from the lemon into a large bowl of cold water and sit it nearby. Cut each quince into quarters. Peel and core each quarter then slice them in half lengthwise (depending on the thickness of the slices, I sometimes cut them slightly smaller for the tart). Drop them into the bowl of lemon water as you go. Don't worry if the quince slices become quite oxidised and brownish, the lemon water prevents this to some extent, but not entirely. However, once they're cooked, it disappears.

Pour 3 cups (750ml) of cold water into a medium–large saucepan, then sit the pan over medium heat. Add the sugar, lemon and mandarin zests and vanilla bean to the saucepan and stir constantly until the sugar has completely dissolved.

Drain the quince and rinse them under cool water. Add them to the pan and bring the liquid to the boil, then reduce the heat to very low. Simmer the quince, covered, for 2½–3 hours or until rosy and tender, carefully turning the top ones once or twice so they cook evenly.

When the quince slices are ready, remove the pan from the heat and leave them to cool in their syrup. By now, they should be the most glorious rosy-pink colour. Carefully transfer the quinces and syrup to a container with a tight-fitting lid, seal it, and store the quinces in the fridge. They will keep well for at least 3 weeks.

# Quince and hazelnut tart

SERVES 12–16

8–10 quince slices from the
slow-cooked vanilla quinces
(see recipe, page 63)
icing sugar, for dusting,
optional

## PASTRY

350g plain flour
100g icing sugar mixture
¼ teaspoon salt
180g cold unsalted butter,
cut into smallish pieces
4 egg yolks

## HAZELNUT FILLING

350g unsalted butter, at room
temperature
350g caster sugar
3 × 60g eggs, at room
temperature
1½ teaspoons vanilla extract
250g hazelnut meal
100g coarsely chopped
roasted hazelnuts
1 tablespoon plain flour

I love this particular combination of flavours, however,
if quinces aren't in season, uncooked just-ripe pears
are lovely, instead. This makes a rather large tart, but
leftovers keep beautifully for up to one week.

For the pastry, tip the flour, icing sugar mixture and salt
into a large food processor fitted with the steel blade. Whiz
them together for about 15 seconds until they're thoroughly
mixed. Stop the processor and dot the butter over the top
of the flour mixture. Whiz again until the mixture resembles
coarse breadcrumbs. Finally, lightly whisk together 3 of the
egg yolks (reserving the last for glazing), then with the motor
running, drizzle them in through the feed tube. Continue
to process the pastry until it comes together to form a ball
around the blade. You may need to stop the processor once
or twice to push the dough onto the blade if it isn't clumping.

Tip the pastry out onto your benchtop and shape into a
20cm-long log. Wrap it in cling film and pop it in the fridge
for about 1½ hours or until it's firm enough to grate (if you
like, you can make the pastry to this point and keep it in the
fridge for a couple of days.)

Sit a 28cm loose-based tart tin (with sides about 3cm
high) on a baking sheet. Use the side of a box grater with the
largest holes to grate the dough onto a plate. I tend to do this
in batches as the grater fills quite quickly. As you finish each
batch, transfer the grated dough to the prepared tin. When
you have finished grating, press the dough strands firmly
and evenly over the base and up the sides of the tin. I find the
easiest way to approach this is to do the sides first and work
my way in. If you like, roll a tumbler over it to flatten it a little
more. Chill for 30 minutes or so, until the pastry is firm.

Preheat your oven to 180°C. To blind bake the shell,
completely cover the pastry with a large sheet of foil,
pressing it gently down into the corners. Spread baking
weights, uncooked rice or dried beans all over the base to
about 1cm-deep. Slide the baking tray into the oven and
bake the tart shell for 25 minutes or until it's set and light
brown. Take it out of the oven and carefully remove the foil
and weights. Beat the remaining egg yolk with 2 teaspoons
of cool water and brush this mixture over the pastry, making
sure it's well coated, then return the tart shell to the oven for
a few minutes so the egg wash sets (this helps seal the pastry
and stop the base becoming soggy once it's filled.) When it's
set, remove the tart shell from the oven and leave it to cool
in the tin on its baking sheet.

Reduce your oven temperature to 150°C. Remove about
8–10 quince slices from their liquid, sit them on paper
towels and pat them dry. If the slices are thick, halve them

lengthwise to help stop them completely sinking into the hazelnut filling.

For the hazelnut filling, beat the butter and sugar in an electric mixer on medium speed for about 3 minutes or until the mixture is pale and light. Beat in the eggs, one at a time, making sure each one is incorporated before adding the next. Reduce the mixer speed to low and add the vanilla, hazelnut meal, chopped hazelnuts and flour. Gently mix them in, scraping down the sides once or twice as you go. Dollop the filling into the tart shell and use a palette knife to spread it out evenly. Gently sit the quince slices on the filling (they will sink down into it as the tart bakes).

Slide the tart, still on its baking sheet, into the oven and bake for about 1¼ hours or until the filling is set in the middle. Once the top is a lovely brown colour, cover it loosely with foil to stop it from darkening any further.

When the tart is ready, put it on a rack and leave it to cool in the tin. To serve, gently pop up the base of the tin and with the help of a wide palette knife, transfer the tart to a serving plate. Dust the top with icing sugar, if using.

# Dark chocolate and halvah semifreddo

I've decided there are two sorts of people in this world. There are those who absolutely adore chocolate with a passion and can eat it any time of the day or night. Then there are those who really can't get quite so excited about it (I realise this attitude is totally inexplicable to chocoholics!). I tend to put myself in the latter category (I'm a caramel girl from way back), but every now and then I taste a chocolate cake or chocolate dessert that gives me cause to rethink where I stand.

My dear friend, Kathy, makes the most amazing chocolate roulade that I've ever tasted. She uses really dark chocolate in the batter with tangy crème fraîche and raspberries to balance out its richness, and it's astoundingly good. This simple chocolate and pistachio halvah semifreddo is another winner. I can always happily have my arm twisted to come back for seconds. The satiny mousse is offset by addictive little nuggets of halvah buried in it like treasure (I love their crisp, sandy texture). I know it looks rather swish, but this gorgeous dessert belies its looks, as it's actually very straightforward to make. It only has five ingredients – cream, chocolate, halvah, vanilla and pistachios. I tend to serve it with fruit on the side to cut through its sweetness, something a bit tangy or sharp like raspberries, roasted apricots or roasted rhubarb. I hope you enjoy it!

Happy Sunday. Belinda ♥

*The satiny mousse is offset by addictive little nuggets of halvah buried in it like treasure.*

## Dark chocolate and halvah semifreddo

SERVES 4–6 (AT A PINCH)

600ml thickened cream
250g good-quality dark
  chocolate, chopped into
  small pieces
200g pistachio halvah
2 teaspoons vanilla extract
2 tablespoons slivered
  pistachio nuts

Line a medium-size loaf tin with baking paper and pop it in the freezer to chill. Make sure the baking paper extends beyond the edges of the tin, so you can use it to help ease the semifreddo out once it's frozen.

Put the cream and chopped chocolate into a large, heavy-based saucepan over very low heat. Warm the mixture, stirring it very regularly (ideally with a flat sauce whisk as this gets right into the corners of the pan), until the chocolate has melted and the mixture is thick and smooth. Don't let it get too hot (not remotely near the boil) or the texture will change. Remove the pan from the heat before the last few pieces of chocolate have melted as the residual heat tends to do this perfectly.

Pour the chocolate mixture into a large bowl and leave it to cool. Pop it into the fridge and let it chill, stirring it regularly as you don't want it to set.

Meanwhile, cut or break the halvah into small pieces. It will crumble as you do this and you'll end up with a range of sizes. Spread them out thinly on a flat plate or baking sheet lined with baking paper and pop it in the freezer.

Once the chocolate mixture is chilled, add the vanilla and use a hand-held electric beater on medium speed to beat until it becomes thick and creamy-looking, but not stiff, or it will develop a slightly grainy texture. I tend to stop using the electric beater a bit before it's ready and finish off by hand with a balloon whisk, so I have more control over the final texture (or, if you'd rather, you can give your arm a workout and use a balloon whisk all the way through). Gently fold the halvah pieces and 1 tablespoon of the slivered pistachios into the chocolate mixture, then spoon it into the prepared tin. You can level the top if you like, but I love the voluptuous curves and wonky top that spooning it in gives the finished loaf. Alternatively, you can scrape it into a container with a tight-fitting lid and serve it in scoops once it's frozen. Scatter the remaining slivered pistachio nuts over the top and pop it in the freezer overnight.

To serve the semifreddo, use the baking paper to help ease it out of the tin, then cut it into thick slices. Serve on chilled plates. It's best eaten within the first few days of making, so the halvah retains its crisp texture, although it's still perfectly delicious long after that, but the halvah will soften.

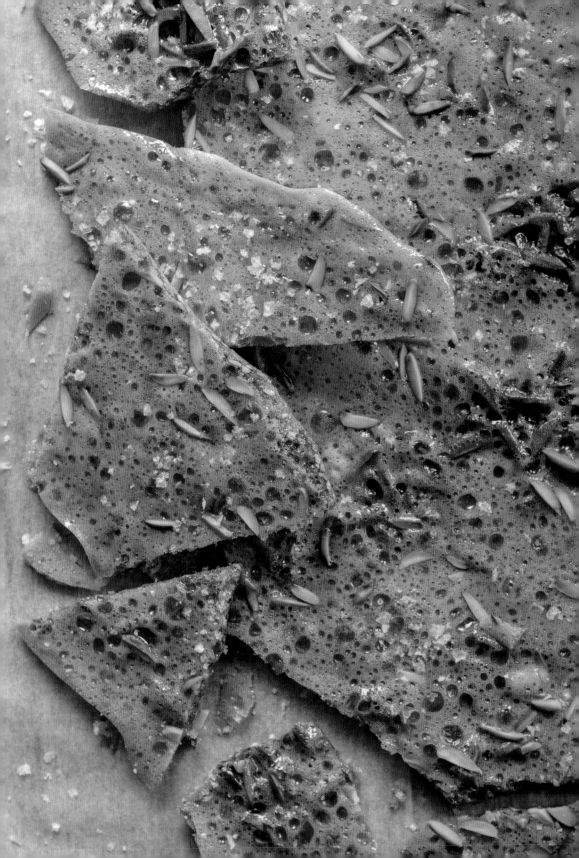

# Salted pistachio brittle

It's about 6am and I'm sitting here with my first cup of tea of the day beside me (it's always the best, isn't it?), the sound of gentle rain on the roof, and I'm looking out onto a gloriously soggy garden – I can't think of a better start to my day.

Earlier this week, I was asked to fill out a questionnaire for an article and one question has stuck in my mind – why are you passionate about cooking? I actually find it quite hard to articulate just why I've devoted the last 40 years to doing what I do, there are so many facets to it. However, after a really wonderful class yesterday, I think I'm closer to being able to answer that question, certainly for the stage I'm now at in my life. As I looked around the kitchen and saw the smiling faces, listened to the chat and laughter as everyone cooked together, watched the delight as new skills were learnt, or when that special 'aha! That's how you do it!' moment occurred, I realised yet again, the great power food and cooking have to bring people, often disparate people, together. Later, as we sat around the table, passing dishes from person to person, tasting and exclaiming about all we had cooked, swapping stories and sharing tales of our lives, and vowing to meet up again at the same time next year, I felt a quiet joy. I had my own private 'aha!' moment. This is the essence of why I do what I do. Yes, some of it is about passing on skills and the joy of cooking, but it's so much more than that and it's a real privilege to be able to do it.

Happy Sunday. Belinda

*Earlier this week, I was asked to fill out a questionnaire for an article and one question has stuck in my mind – why are you passionate about cooking?*

# Salted pistachio brittle

SERVES 8–10

1 cup (220g) caster sugar
½ cup (180g) clear honey
100g slivered pistachio nuts
15g unsalted butter
1 teaspoon sea salt flakes,
    plus extra, for sprinkling
¾ teaspoon bicarbonate
    of soda

The technique for making this brittle is similar to that used in making honeycomb. Bicarbonate of soda is stirred into a golden toffee mixture, which immediately bubbles up and becomes very light. I use it to decorate all sorts of cakes – it looks lovely finely chopped and sprinkled over or around the edge of a cake or broken into shards and scattered or pressed into the icing. Be warned, its salty caramel flavour and crunchy texture make it totally addictive!

Line a large, shallow baking tray with baking paper and sit it on a board, wire rack or thick tea towel.

Pour the sugar, honey and ¼ cup (60ml) water into a medium–large saucepan and sit it over medium heat. Stir constantly until the sugar has dissolved, then stop stirring, increase the heat a little and bring the mixture to the boil. If you have one, clip a sugar thermometer to the side of the pan and let the mixture cook, undisturbed, washing down the sides occasionally with a brush dipped in water to dissolve any sugar crystals. The mixture will gradually change from being liquid to syrupy with lots of lazy bubbles breaking all over the surface.

From here on in you need to watch it like a hawk, as it changes colour quite rapidly. As soon as the thermometer reaches 140°C (this is also known as 'soft crack' stage), stir in the slivered pistachios, butter and sea salt (if you don't have a thermometer, at this point the mixture will be a pale gold colour). Continue to cook the syrup, stirring regularly, until the thermometer registers just over 150°C ('hard crack' stage) and the nuts are golden. The caramel, too, should be a lovely golden brown – just remember it will darken a little as it cools. Sprinkle the bicarbonate of soda over the mixture and stir quickly to mix it in – the mixture will puff up and become lighter with a honeycomb-like texture.

Immediately take the pan off the heat and carefully pour the mixture onto the prepared baking tray. Using oven gloves to protect your hands, tilt the tray gently to help spread the mixture even further or use a palette knife or heatproof spatula to spread it out. Be careful doing this, as both the brittle and tray are very hot. Finally, sprinkle some extra sea salt over the top, then leave the brittle to cool completely and harden.

To serve, break it into shards or chop it coarsely. To store the shards, layer them in an airtight container between sheets of baking paper or freezer wrap to stop them sticking together, then pop them in the freezer until you need them. The brittle will keep well for 1 month or more.

*Sunday 26<sup>th</sup> April*

# Gigantes plaki
# (Greek-style baked beans)

Every now and then, I get a bee in my bonnet about certain recipes, which I make again and again trying to get them 'just so'. It will often be the case that I'm attempting to recreate a dish I've eaten, the flavour memory of which stays in my mind. This can be both a good and a bad thing – I know how I'd like the dish to taste, but there can be a lot of trial and error getting to that point! I've recently gone down such a rabbit hole with a dish of beans.

It all started because we often share meals with our lovely neighbour, Diane, a wonderful horticulturalist who also happens to be a fabulous cook. More often than not we have a potluck meal, where we each cook something and then sit around the table eating, laughing and catching up. I look forward to these evenings, not only for the wide-ranging conversations, but also for the delicious dishes she cooks.

*OMG, those beans were so delicious – moist, meaty and fragrant with olive oil, dill and tomatoes.*

Well, last week Di arrived with an earthenware bowl full of beautiful slow-cooked lima beans (she grows the beans herself and calls them her Jack and the Beanstalk beans). OMG, they were *so* delicious – moist, meaty and fragrant with olive oil, dill and tomatoes. Just one taste took me back to our first visit to Greece, when I was in my early twenties and we travelled and lived in a Kombi van, surviving on the smell of an oily rag. Occasionally, as a treat we would visit a local taverna and eat nourishing bowlsful of beans (gigantes) just like the ones Di cooked. Needless to say, I'm now deep down that rabbit hole trying to replicate them. This recipe, based on Diane's, is the result of numerous attempts to make them and is as close as I can get to those I remember. They're delicious just as is. Or, as Di does when she serves them, they're better still with a little feta sprinkled over the top when they're reheated. They're also brilliant for brunch, topped with poached eggs and trickled with a little chilli oil – a few chorizo sausages alongside don't go amiss, either!

Happy Sunday. Belinda ♥

# Gigantes plaki (Greek-style baked beans)

SERVES 8

500g dried lima beans
4 cloves garlic, bruised
200ml extra-virgin olive oil,
    plus extra, for drizzling
2 onions, finely chopped
3 carrots, finely chopped
3 large stalks celery, finely
    diced
3 cloves garlic, extra, finely
    chopped
2–3 small red chillies, finely
    chopped, optional
1kg ripe tomatoes
2 bay leaves
1 large thyme sprig
1 teaspoon sea salt flakes
freshly ground black pepper
1 small bunch dill, finely
    chopped
3 teaspoons brown sugar
1 tablespoon balsamic vinegar
feta or marinated goat's
    cheese, to serve, optional

This recipe makes rather a lot of beans, however, they keep beautifully in the fridge for up to a week and go with all sorts of things, such as barbecued meats, eggs, and spicy sausages, or they make a lovely meal on their own with a handful of spinach leaves mixed in when you reheat them. Just be mindful of one thing, please, don't skimp on the olive oil, it makes all the difference to the flavour. The variety of lima beans I love to use when I can get my hands on them are the lovely speckled ones, known as Madagascar running beans.

Rinse the beans thoroughly under cold, running water, then tip them into a large bowl. Cover them with a generous amount of cool water (they will drink it up), cover the bowl and leave them in a cool spot overnight to swell.

The next day, drain the beans and tip them into a large saucepan. Completely cover them with cold water, sit the pan over high heat and bring them to the boil. Reduce the heat so they bubble steadily for 10 minutes, then drain again. Return them to the pan along with the bruised garlic, pour in a fresh lot of water to cover to the depth of 5cm and return to the heat. Let them bubble gently, occasionally skimming any impurities from the surface, until they're tender. The time for this can vary greatly depending on how fresh the beans are – I usually start checking after 1 hour, but they could take another half-hour or so. The only way to check properly is to fish a couple out, blow on them to cool and then eat them. Once they're ready, drain, but keep ½ cup (125ml) of their cooking water.

Heat the oil in a large, flameproof dish over medium heat (I use an enamelled cast iron pan for this). Add the onion and cook for 10 minutes, stirring occasionally, and adjusting the heat so they're translucent-looking but don't colour much. Add the carrot, celery, chopped garlic, and chilli, if using, and continue to cook for another 10 minutes or until the vegetables have softened a little.

Meanwhile, sit a box grater on a large plate. Halve the tomatoes and grate them with the cut-side of the tomato facing the coarsest side of the grater – they will become mushy and pureed as you grate. You should just be left with the skin in your fingers, which you can discard.

Add the grated tomato, bay leaves, thyme, salt and pepper to the vegetables, reduce the heat to low and cook, stirring occasionally, for 1 hour. After this time, remove the pan from the heat and discard the bay leaves and thyme (I sometimes hang onto a bay leaf to use as a garnish). Now, Di likes to puree her sauce at this stage, as she finds it clings more to the beans, but if you'd like it a bit chunkier, just leave it as is.

Preheat your oven to 180°C. Add the cooked lima beans, dill (reserving a few sprigs for garnishing, if you like), brown sugar, and balsamic vinegar to the tomato mixture and thoroughly mix them in. Cover the dish and pop it into the oven for 1 hour. When they're ready, remove the dish from the oven and let the beans cool a little before serving. It's a good idea to taste them and add a little salt or splash of the reserved bean cooking water if the mixture seems a bit thick.

Serve in the dish or transfer to a serving dish, drizzle with a little olive oil, then sprinkle with feta (or goat's cheese) and reserved dill sprigs or bay leaf, if using.

# MAY

Smoked salmon, caper, dill and goat's cheese tart

Simple shortcrust pastry tart shell

My lumberjack cake

Orange syrup cake with lemon-scented cream and sugared almonds

A beautiful green salad with my favourite salad dressing

Warm olives with garlic and herbs

# Smoked salmon, caper, dill and goat's cheese tart

One savoury tart = three local growers. Maths was never my strong point, but this is an equation I do understand!

Yesterday, as I was making a smoked salmon tart with leftover pastry from my classes, I found myself smiling as I counted the different local farmers whose ingredients had gone into making it. There was beautiful milk, crème fraîche and marinated feta from Debra Allard of Cheeses Loves You. Debra, an award-winning cheesemaker, and her husband, Jim, have a herd of much-loved Jersey cows, whose milk is used to make her wonderful cheeses, yoghurt, buttermilk and dairy products. I love visiting her stall at the farmers market as there is always laughter ringing out from it and many Very Important Discussions being had about which cheese to choose. There were fragrant, rusty-coloured kampot peppercorns and hand-picked capers from growers extraordinaire, John (pictured opposite) and Lyndall Picone from Picone Exotics, who live close by and grow all sorts of glorious fruits. The eggs, which made a custard so golden it looked as though it had been infused with saffron, were from the gorgeous heirloom chooks raised just up the road by Obi and Ash of Good Goog Eggs. There were also bunches of chives and dill from our garden. I'm not hugely green-fingered, but just growing these few additions makes me feel incredibly productive.

I can't tell you the pleasure this simple calculation gave me. I feel so very fortunate to be able to cook beautiful fresh produce like this, grown locally by people I know and admire. Their efforts and work inform and inspire everything I do in my writing and my classes, and I'm so very grateful to them.

Happy Sunday. Belinda 💜

*One savoury tart = three local growers. I can't tell you the pleasure this simple calculation gave me.*

# Smoked salmon, caper, dill and goat's cheese tart

SERVES 6-8

1 blind-baked 25–26cm shortcrust pastry tart shell, in its tin (see recipe, page 84)

5 × 60g eggs

300ml milk

150ml cream (sour cream or crème fraîche)

1 teaspoon sea salt flakes

¼ teaspoon freshly ground nutmeg

good grinding of black peppercorns

2 tablespoons finely chopped dill

2 tablespoons finely chopped chives

200g smoked salmon, torn into bite-size pieces

1½ tablespoons capers (salted, if possible)

100g (or so) soft feta or marinated goat's cheese, drained and lightly crushed

herb sprigs and leaves, to garnish

This is wonderful served with a salad that includes fennel, as the two go beautifully together.

Preheat your oven to 175°C. Sit the tart tin with the cooked pastry shell on a baking sheet and set it aside.

In a large bowl, lightly whisk the eggs with a balloon whisk to break them up. Add the milk, cream, salt, nutmeg and pepper and whisk everything thoroughly together. Stir in the dill and chives. Pour the mixture into a jug, cover it and put it in the fridge until you're ready to use it. You can do this a couple of hours ahead of time, if you like.

When you're ready to bake the tart, strew the smoked salmon, capers, and feta or goat's cheese evenly over the base of the tart. Give the egg mixture another quick whisk as it will have settled somewhat, then pour it into the tart shell. I usually do this right by the oven or put the baking sheet with the tart shell on the partly pulled-out oven shelf before pouring in the liquid, as it's easy to spill if you carry the tray any distance, which I've learnt the hard way!

Slide the baking sheet with the tart carefully into the oven. Cook for about 35 minutes or until the filling is set but still a little wobbly. The best way to check this is to very lightly rest the palm of your hand on the filling and give it a gentle jiggle. Remove the tart from the oven and leave it to settle in the tin for 5 minutes or so. It's also lovely served just-warm.

To serve, remove the outer ring of the tart tin, then use a long palette knife to help slide the tart off the base and onto a serving platter. Strew fresh herb sprigs and leaves over the top.

## A NOTE ABOUT OVENS

I can bang on endlessly about ovens! I think they're the bane of a recipe writer's life, as it seems to me that no two ovens are calibrated in quite the same way. At the end of the day, the most important thing is to get to know your own oven, with all its foibles, as this will make life much easier for you and allow you to adjust temperatures if necessary.

The thermostat of my oven can be dodgy, so I always use an oven thermometer to check the temperature accurately. If you're concerned that your oven may be a bit unreliable, then one of these can be a blessing.

There's also the question of fan-forced ovens. Like regular ovens, these vary enormously. If you're baking with the fan on, be aware that everything will cook faster and hotter, which means it has the potential to burn and dry out more quickly, so it's a good idea to reduce the recommended oven temperature by 10°C, and to start checking whatever you're cooking a little earlier than the recipe says.

## Simple shortcrust pastry tart shell

MAKES 1 × 26–28CM ROUND
TART SHELL OR 1 × 30CM × 21CM
RECTANGULAR TART SHELL

1½ cups (225g) plain flour
¼ teaspoon salt
125g cold unsalted butter,
    cut into small pieces
1 egg yolk (from 60g egg)
    mixed with 2 teaspoons cold
    water, for glazing

This is the pastry recipe that I use all the time – it makes terrific pastry that's short and buttery without being too difficult to handle. In fact, over the years I've noticed that many of my students who have sworn off ever making pastry, have actually become remarkably adept once they try this recipe. So even if you feel a little nervous about making it, please give it a go, it really does work well.

I've been racking my brains about what the most important tips are that I can pass on to you. One in particular that keeps surfacing is just what a difference it makes when you get a handle on when pastry is at the right stage for rolling. It's not hard to pick this up, however, you may have to make it a few times before you feel entirely comfortable with it. Basically, if the pastry seems too soft to roll, chill it a bit longer; if it's hard and cracks around the edges as you begin to flatten it, then let it soften a bit more. The temperature of the room where you're rolling the pastry also makes a difference. Pastry is always much easier to handle when the weather is cooler, as it softens rapidly in warm weather. Having said that, I live in a near-tropical climate and still make it – so there is hope! I tend to roll it early in the morning before the temperature soars and also try to work quite quickly to prevent it becoming too warm and soft.

Whiz the flour and salt together in a food processor. Add the butter and whiz until the mixture resembles medium breadcrumbs. With the motor running, pour in ¼ cup (60ml) iced water and process only until the dough forms a ball around the blade. The time for this varies depending on the weather; when it's warm it comes together faster.

Tip the dough out onto a board and shape it into a ball. Now, flatten it into a disc and wrap tightly in cling film. Chill the disc in the fridge for about 40 minutes or until the pastry is firm but supple enough to roll out. By the way, if you want to make the pastry ahead of time, it keeps well in the fridge for up to 3 days, but it will be too firm to roll at this stage, so let it warm up at room temperature until it's pliable. (You can also make the pastry a few weeks ahead and freeze it, then just defrost it in the fridge overnight.)

On a lightly floured board, roll out the pastry to a large round to fit a 26–28cm loose-based tart tin (or use a 30cm × 21cm rectangular tin, as I did). Roll the pastry over your rolling pin to transfer it to the tin. Then gently drape it over the tin, being careful you don't press down on the sharp edges, which may cut through it.

Use your knuckles to gently press the pastry into the tin, leaving an overhang all around. Trim a little pastry from the

overhang and keep it in the fridge in case you need to patch any cracks later on. Sit the tin on a baking tray (this makes it much easier to manoeuvre both now and later when the tart is baking) and chill for 40 minutes or until the pastry is firm.

Preheat your oven to 200°C. Completely cover the pastry with a large sheet of foil, pressing it gently down into the corners. Spread baking weights, uncooked rice or dried beans all over the base to a depth of about 1cm.

Slide the baking tray into the oven and bake the tart shell for 20 minutes or until it's nearly set. Remove it from the oven and run a rolling pin over the foil on the top edge to cut off the pastry overhang. Return the tin to the oven with the foil and weights still intact and bake the pastry for another 10 minutes or until it's lightly coloured and feels firm and dry. Take it out again and carefully remove the foil and weights. Don't worry if there are any fine cracks in the shell, just patch them with the reserved pastry.

Brush the egg yolk mixture over the pastry, making sure it is well coated, then return the tart shell to the oven for a few minutes so the egg wash sets to a shiny glaze. If you're wondering what the egg wash does, it's to help seal the pastry by filling in any hairline cracks, forming a lacquer-like layer between the crust and filling, which in turn, helps prevent the filling leaking into the base and making it soggy.

When it's set, remove the tart shell from the oven and leave it to cool in the tin on a rack. It's then ready to be filled.

**P.S.** If you would rather higher sides and a fluted rim for your tart, you need to do things a little differently. Once you've lined the tin with pastry, trim off the excess with a sharp knife but leave a 2cm border all the way around. Turn this border inwards, slightly over on itself and then pinch it so it sits up higher than the rim of the tin. If you like, flute the edge by pinching it gently between your thumb and forefinger. To blind bake it, line the tin as above with the foil and baking weights, but leave them intact for the full 30 minutes cooking time. Then continue with the glaze.

*Sunday 10<sup>th</sup> May*

# My lumberjack cake

Although my mum died many years ago, I'm more aware than ever of the profound impact she's had on my daily life. I find myself emulating many of the small everyday things she used to do – there were always fresh flowers floating in a shallow bowl by the front door to welcome people to our home; there was always room for one more person at the dinner table; a meal for five could easily stretch to feed ten; simple, wholesome food, cooked and served with care, is an important part of daily life (and yes, that means napkins and some garden flowers on the table, even if it is just for macaroni cheese). A proper handwritten thank you note is non-negotiable (I'm afraid I've lapsed a bit on this and send out emails, too, but I do try!).

The little dictums. If you can't say anything nice about someone, don't say anything at all. Don't take people at face value. Everyone has a story. There is always solace to be found by getting your hands in the soil. And then there are her expressions, which I use to this day.

"I look like the wreck of the Hesperus!" Which, I have to admit, I do some days after hours spent in the garden. "I'm up to dolly's wax!" I'm definitely known to say this when I've eaten too much.

These are all small things but precious, and I'm so grateful for them.

I look at my hands now – age spots and all – and recall her lamenting how hers had changed, and find myself doing the same thing. If I close my eyes I can feel the sense of love, care and warmth that she extended to everyone who entered our home – our friends all adored her. Always gracious, always kind, always caring, even when dementia stole away the final years of her life.

And there's one other dictum that I've happily stuck to – there must always be homemade cake for afternoon tea. So, Mum, in your honour, I'm baking this cake for afternoon tea today. It has caramel and nuts – the two things you loved most.

To those of you who are mums, I hope you have a really happy day. To those, like me, who miss your mums sorely, I hope you find a few moments today to sit quietly and enjoy cherished memories of your own mum.

Happy Mother's Day. Belinda 🖤

*If I close my eyes I can feel the sense of love, care and warmth that she extended to everyone who entered our home – our friends all adored her. Always gracious, always kind, always caring, even when dementia stole away the final years of her life.*

# My lumberjack cake

SERVES 8-10

300g (about 2 medium-size)
sweet apples, peeled, cored
and cut into 1cm pieces
200g pitted dates, finely
chopped
1 teaspoon bicarbonate
of soda
1 cup (150g) plain flour, plus
extra, for dusting
½ cup (75g) self-raising flour
½ teaspoon salt
125g unsalted butter, at room
temperature
1 cup (220g) caster sugar
1 × 60g egg
1½ teaspoons vanilla extract
50g roasted pecans or
almonds, coarsely chopped
softly whipped cream or
good-quality vanilla
ice-cream, to serve

**TOPPING**
90g unsalted butter
½ cup (125ml) milk
½ cup (110g) soft brown sugar
¼ cup (60g) dark brown sugar
110g flaked almonds or sliced
pecans
1 teaspoon vanilla extract

This luscious and surprisingly light cake is chock-full of apple and dates. The thing I most love about it is the slightly toffeed caramel and nut topping, as I'm an absolute push-over when it comes to anything with caramel in it. Gala, pink lady, and fuji apples all work well for this cake.

Preheat your oven to 180°C. Butter a 20cm springform cake tin, line the base with buttered baking paper and dust the tin with flour.

Put the apple into a heatproof bowl with the dates. Add the bicarbonate of soda and pour in 1 cup (250ml) boiling water. Thoroughly stir everything together, then leave the mixture to cool to room temperature.

Tip both flours and the salt into a separate bowl and whisk them together with a balloon whisk for 1 minute so they're well combined. Set the bowl aside.

Scoop the butter and caster sugar into the bowl of an electric mixer with the paddle attachment and beat on medium speed for 4–5 minutes or until they're light and fluffy. Then, with the motor running, beat in the egg and vanilla extract. Reduce the speed to the lowest setting and add the flour mixture, alternating with the apple and date mixture, until they're both incorporated. Take care not to overdo this mixing or the cake may be a bit tough. Lastly, stir in the nuts.

Scrape the batter into the prepared cake tin and bake for 1¼ hours or until a fine skewer inserted into the middle comes out slightly moist. (I know this isn't the usual instruction for testing a cake with a skewer, normally you would check that the skewer comes out clean, however in this case, the topping is spread onto the cake and then it goes back into the oven again to finish baking.)

When the cake is nearly ready, make the topping. Heat the butter and milk in a small saucepan over medium heat. As soon as the butter melts, stir in both the sugars, the flaked almonds or sliced pecans, and vanilla extract. Adjust the heat so the mixture bubbles steadily, and cook, stirring regularly, for 5 minutes or until it's slightly thickened. Keep the mixture in a warm spot until you're ready to use it.

Remove the cake from the oven and sit it on a wire rack. Use the back of a spoon to firmly but carefully flatten the top so that it's as level as possible. Scrape the warm topping mixture onto the cake and use a palette knife to spread it out evenly. A little of the topping will run down the sides of the pan, but this is fine (in fact, it makes for some divine chewy caramel bits). Pop the cake back into the oven for 10–15 minutes or until the topping is deep golden brown.

The topping may leak a tiny bit through the seal on the tin, so it's a good idea to sit a sheet of baking paper under the cake to catch any drips.

Sit the cake on a wire rack and leave it to cool completely in the tin. When you're ready to serve, carefully loosen the cake from the sides of the tin with a fine palette knife. Sit a sheet of baking paper on top of the cake (this helps keep the top from being damaged), and invert it onto the rack. Remove the tin, then invert the cake again onto a serving plate. Serve with whipped cream or vanilla ice-cream.

**P.S.** If the topping looks a little pale when you lift the cake out of the oven, carefully run the cake, in its tin, under a hot grill to brown the top a little more before leaving it to cool on the rack.

*Sunday 17<sup>th</sup> May*

# Orange syrup cake with lemon-scented cream and sugared almonds

Brrrr! The Arctic weather from down south arrived here with a vengeance overnight. When I finally stirred up the courage to get out of bed, I grabbed my tablet to write this, and buried myself back under the covers again. So, I'm tapping away with the blankets pulled up to the tip of my nose, a pair of long-forgotten mittens on my hands (thank goodness I kept them) and I'm sending subliminal messages to my husband who is fast asleep beside me (he doesn't feel the cold and walks around all winter in a T-shirt when everyone else is rugged up to the nines) that a pot of tea would be most welcome. Fingers crossed it works!

It's not very often that I get the chance to cook purely for pleasure, but this week, I've had the best time 'playing' in my kitchen. I've not been cooking under any pressure or to a deadline, just cooking for the joy of it. I've made dinner for a dear friend's birthday, tried new recipes for my classes, made jars and jars of marmalade and preserved lemons, and attempted a cake, the idea for which has been buzzing around in my head for ages. I'm very happy to say it worked! So, meet my new favourite – a golden orange syrup cake with lemon cream and sugared almonds. It's a definite on the cooking class menu for the next few months and last night it made the prettiest birthday cake scattered with tiny chamomile flowers.

That's it from me this morning, my darling husband is still in the land of nod, so I'm going to have to brave the icy blast and make that cuppa myself. I hope you stay warm and cosy and have a lovely day.

Happy Sunday. Belinda ♥

*I'm tapping away writing this with the blankets pulled up to the tip of my nose, and a pair of long-forgotten mittens on my hands.*

## Orange syrup cake with lemon-scented cream and sugared almonds

SERVES 10–12

225g unsalted butter,
  plus extra, for greasing
170g plain flour
2½ teaspoons baking powder
¼ teaspoon salt
225g icing sugar mixture,
  sifted
3 × 60g eggs, lightly beaten
100ml freshly squeezed
  orange juice
finely grated zest of 3 large
  oranges
½ teaspoon vanilla extract
  or paste
tiny edible flowers (such as
  chamomile), optional

**LEMON-SCENTED CREAM**

1½ cups (375ml) thickened
  cream
¼ cup (40g) icing sugar, sifted
1 heaped tablespoon finely
  grated lemon zest

**SUGARED ALMONDS**

100g flaked almonds
30g caster sugar
3 teaspoons Grand Marnier
  or Cointreau

**ORANGE SYRUP**

100ml freshly squeezed
  orange juice, strained
150g caster sugar
1 tablespoon Grand Marnier
  or Cointreau

Although this cake sounds no different to many others, the texture is really quite perfect. Unusually for a cake like this, the butter is melted before being creamed with the sugar, which gives it a beautiful crumb. Baking the cake in a wide tin also allows the syrup to seep evenly throughout the whole cake, so each slice is very moist. You'll need to make the lemon-scented cream a few hours before you plan to serve the cake. The sugared almonds are entirely optional, but they do look lovely.

For the lemon-scented cream, put the cream, icing sugar and lemon zest into a small saucepan over low heat. Very slowly bring the mixture to just below boiling point – there should be tiny bubbles forming around the edge of the pan. Turn off the heat, cover the pan and leave the cream to cool to room temperature. Once cooled, pour the cream into a container, cover it tightly and put it in the fridge for a few hours or overnight. When you're ready to use the cream, strain it through a fine sieve into a chilled bowl and whip it to soft peaks (if you find the cream has thickened considerably overnight, you may need to use the back of a spoon to help push it through the sieve).

For the sugared almonds, preheat your oven to 150°C. Line a small baking tray with baking paper. Toss all the ingredients together in a bowl to moisten the almonds lightly. Spread the almonds, as best you can, in a single layer on the prepared tray. Slide the tray into the oven and cook the almonds, turning them frequently using a spatula, for about 15–20 minutes or until they're golden and crisp. When they're ready, transfer the tray to a rack and let the almonds cool completely. Sometimes a few clump together, but I rather like this as they look pretty. If not using straightaway, you can store them in an airtight container in the freezer, where they keep well for up to 6 weeks. There is no need to defrost them before using as they warm up quickly.

For the cake, increase your oven temperature to 200°C. Butter a 27–28cm fluted cake tin (it doesn't have to be fluted, but the fluting does look pretty. Just make sure it's not a springform pan with a removable base, as the batter is really runny and will seep out). Line the base with buttered baking paper, dust the tin lightly with flour and set it aside.

Put the butter into a small saucepan and melt over extremely low heat. As soon as the butter is ¾ melted, remove the pan from the heat and set it aside – the remaining butter will melt in the residual heat.

Meanwhile, tip the flour, baking powder and salt into a medium-size bowl and whisk them together with a balloon whisk for 1 minute. Set the bowl aside.

Pour the melted butter into the bowl of an electric mixer (or use a medium-size bowl and a hand-held electric mixer). Add the icing sugar mixture and beat on medium speed for 2–3 minutes or until the mixture looks creamy (don't expect it to be as fluffy as when you cream room temperature butter and sugar). It may initially look separated, but will come together quickly. With the beater going, dribble in the beaten egg, a little at a time. Once this is incorporated, reduce the speed to low, drizzle in the orange juice and continue to beat until it's absorbed (it will be quite splashy at this stage). Add the flour mixture along with the orange zest and vanilla and mix only until just combined – the batter will be surprisingly runny. Alternatively, you can gently stir the flour mixture in by hand, just be careful not to overwork it or the cake may be a bit tough. Pour the batter into the prepared tin.

Bake the cake for 10 minutes, reduce the temperature to 175°C and continue baking for 20–25 minutes or until the cake is golden and gently springs back when lightly pressed in the centre. Alternatively, a toothpick inserted into the centre should come out clean and the cake should come away slightly from the sides of the tin. Transfer the cake to a wire rack and leave it to cool in the tin for 20 minutes.

While the cake is cooling, make the orange syrup. Pour the orange juice and caster sugar into a medium-size saucepan. Sit the pan over medium heat and stir constantly until the sugar is dissolved, then remove the pan from the heat and stir in the liqueur.

Sit a serving plate or cake stand over the cake. Carefully invert the cake and gently remove the tin and paper. Slowly but surely, brush the syrup over the cake until it's all absorbed, then leave the cake to cool completely.

To serve, swoosh the lemon-scented cream over the top of the cake and sprinkle it with the sugared almonds. Scatter with edible flowers, if you have some.

# A beautiful green salad with my favourite salad dressing

When I'm teaching, I rarely get the chance to stand back and look around at the class. But one such moment occurred yesterday, and as I took in what was happening, I couldn't help but smile. The kitchen was full of laughter as eight very busy participants, chopped, sautéed, kneaded and whisked their way through the day. Bowls and baskets brimmed with autumn produce – pale green cobs of just-picked corn; knobbly jicama bulbs, their unassuming exterior hiding their sweet, crunchy flesh; extraordinary red- and white-flecked peanuts from my dear friend Palisa; stems of fleshy purslane leaves; Meyer lemons from our tree (says she, very proudly); our beautiful rainbow eggs; the tiniest, sweetest heads of cos; a box of extraordinary mushrooms from the farmers market, which we all oohed and aahed over; while limes, oranges and mandarins rubbed shoulders with fragrant quinces waiting to be transformed into a ruby bowlful of lusciousness (see recipe, page 63). It was such a joy to see. My husband, Clive – who also happens to be my EA, recipe taster, roadie, and dishwasher extraordinaire – had just swapped hats to barista mode to help keep us going. Meanwhile, our wonderful helper, Laura, was dashing between sink, fridge and cooktop. Flowers – sweetly-scented waterlilies, cheerful zinnias and golden tarragon blooms – brightened every corner. And do you know what? I felt so happy and proud of what we do in this lovely old hall. I know that people come to be taught by me, but believe me, it really is a team effort to create these special days, starting with the farmers and their beautiful produce, Laura (and before Laura, Sue, and Belle), and Clive and the incredible amount of work they do, and our participants, who come from near and far to be here with us. A big thank you to you all. I don't know how long we shall continue to do it, but while we do, I just feel so proud of what we've all created.

Happy Sunday. Belinda ♥

*The kitchen was full of laughter as eight very busy participants chopped, sautéed, kneaded and whisked their way through the day.*

# A beautiful green salad with my favourite salad dressing

SERVES 6

300g mixed salad greens
1 large ripe avocado, sliced
    or diced, optional
1 large handful roasted nuts,
    whole or coarsely chopped

### DRESSING

1 very small eschalot, very
    finely chopped (or the pale
    green and white parts of
    1 medium-size spring onion)
1–1½ tablespoons aged sherry
    vinegar, or more to taste
1 cup (250ml) extra-virgin
    olive oil
2–3 teaspoons Dijon mustard
1½ teaspoons honey, or more
    to taste
1 very small clove garlic,
    finely chopped
1 teaspoon sea salt flakes,
    or more to taste

The secret of a really sensational simple green salad is always in the dressing. The greens you use can vary widely according to the time of year and they will add their own personality to the salad – peppery, bitter, buttery, nutty, crunchy, tender, and crisp – but it's the dressing, and having nice, dry salad leaves, that are key. Choose a mixture of salad leaves for both flavour and texture, such as rocket, watercress, witlof, iceberg, cos, mignonette, radicchio, friseé, nasturtiums and purslane. For the nuts in this salad pictured, I've used my friend Palisa's lovely red and white peanuts, but pecans or macadamias are also delicious. This particular dressing is my favourite and makes considerably more than you need for this salad, but it keeps well in a tightly sealed jar in the fridge for a couple of weeks.

For the dressing, scrape the chopped eschalot into a fine strainer and rinse quickly under cold water. Set it aside to drain. Press down on it firmly to remove any excess water then scoop it into a medium-size bowl and cover it with the vinegar and 3–4 teaspoons of warm water. Leave it to sit for a couple of minutes before adding the remaining ingredients. Whisk everything together until thoroughly combined and both the honey and salt have dissolved. Taste the dressing and adjust the flavours to suit you. Pour the dressing into a jar, seal it tightly and store it in the fridge. Return to cool room temperature before using.

Remove any damaged or wilted leaves from the greens you're using, then gently wash them in cool water to remove any grit (it's the worst thing to bite into when you're eating a salad, it literally puts your teeth on edge). Dry the greens in batches in a salad spinner, then gently wrap in dry tea towels and chill until ready to use. Alternatively, put them into a large stainless-steel bowl, cover tightly and pop it in the fridge until you're ready for them – they crisp up beautifully.

To serve the salad, add the avocado, if using, to the bowl of greens. With your hands (don a pair of prep gloves, if you like), gently mix the greens in the bowl with some of the dressing until they're glistening and well-coated but not drowned, then pile them into a salad bowl. Sprinkle the nuts over the top to serve.

## Sunday 31<sup>st</sup> May
# Warm olives with garlic and herbs

Olives are a bit of a 'thing' in my family. I think we were pretty much weaned on them. When we were young, my dad would buy them from the only Greek deli within kilometres of home. I remember the big rectangular cans, with their wonderfully exotic labels, were kept on the floor in the pantry and decanted into glass jars to which mum would add herbs and garlic. Actually, I should say that they were *originally* kept on the floor of the pantry, until the day my sister, aged five, helped herself to a big bowlful and disappeared from sight. After hunting for her high and low, she was finally discovered quietly sitting underneath the dining table, scissors in one hand snipping off her beautiful curls, while the other hand dipped repeatedly into the bowl of olives. I suspect she was in a state of olive-induced bliss!

Our love of them appears to have been passed down through the family. As a littlie, my niece coined the name 'olivers' for them, and they've remained 'olivers' to me, ever since. As far as I'm concerned, the best way to eat them is to warm them through with olive oil, garlic and herbs.

If you would like to try a batch of these lovely 'olivers', all you need do is stir together 360g olives (I tend to use a mixture of tiny Niçoise, shiny black Kalamatas, and bright-green Sicilian olives for this, but really, any will do), 8 caperberries (if you have some), 200ml extra-virgin olive oil, a clove of crushed garlic, several sprigs of thyme, rosemary or oregano, and 3 teaspoons of balsamic vinegar. Put everything into a saucepan and very gently heat the mixture until the olives are warm. Turn off the heat and let them sit at cool room temperature for at least 6 hours to allow the flavours to develop. Just before you serve them, gently reheat the olives, then spoon them into a serving bowl. As one of my students said on first tasting them, "I'm never going to eat olives any other way again!".

Happy Sunday. Belinda 💜

*She was finally discovered quietly sitting underneath the dining table, scissors in one hand snipping off her beautiful curls, while the other hand dipped repeatedly into the bowl of olives.*

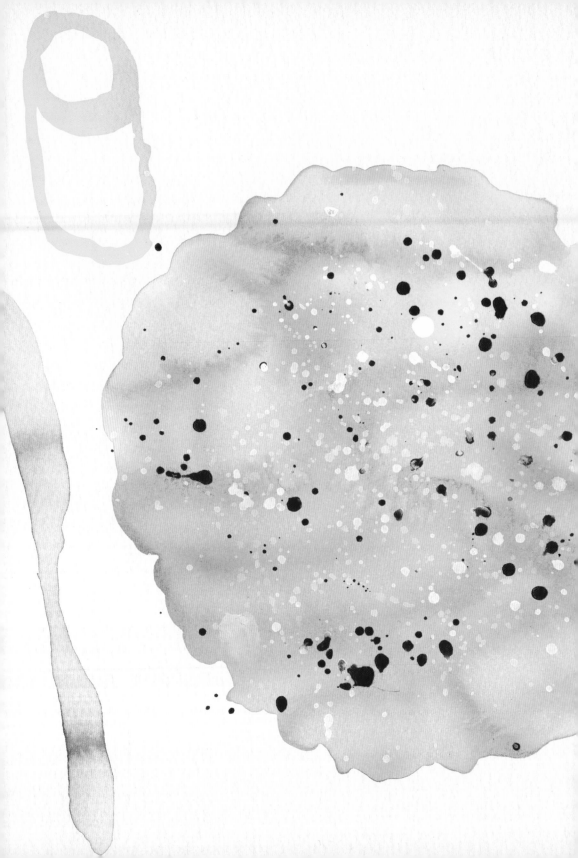

# JUNE

Gently spicy roasted cauliflower soup

Sweetcorn with smoked paprika butter and lime

Lemon curd and shortbread tart

Jalapeños with smoked pancetta and goat's cheese

*Sunday 7<sup>th</sup> June*

# Gently spicy roasted cauliflower soup

I'm convinced I've inherited the washerwoman gene from my mum. Nothing makes me happier than a line of washing blowing merrily in the breeze and nothing delights me more than the crisp fragrance of sun-dried washing as I fold it into the basket. I find myself burying my nose in towels, shirts and pillowslips as I sort them into neat piles. I wish I could say the same about the ironing that goes with it, though. My enthusiasm definitely starts to wane at the prospect of that!

Yesterday, in an effort to stave off my ironing chores a bit longer, I quickly convinced myself that my time would be better spent in the kitchen working on some recipes I've been meaning to try. My starting point for this sort of day is inevitably the farmers market and Friday's market was a cracker! There were freshly dug Dutch cream potatoes, a damp, earthy fragrance still clinging to each one; knobby, fist-size custard apples sitting cheek-by-jowl with mandarins; blowsy red and green cabbages; vibrant bunches of mint and chervil; creamy cauliflowers nestled in their protective leaves; and avocados of every shape and size. Oh, and the best array of salad greens you could ever wish to see. I know it seems a bit counterintuitive to eat salad in winter, but it's when these greens are at their peak, as the chilly air brings out their flavours, and they're a perfect counterpoint to beautiful slow-cooked casseroles, stews and soups, like this gently spicy roasted cauliflower one. Simple meals like this really are my favourite of all.

Happy Sunday. Belinda

*There were freshly dug Dutch cream potatoes, a damp, earthy fragrance still clinging to each one, and cauliflowers nestled in their protective leaves.*

# Gently spicy roasted cauliflower soup

SERVES 4–6

1 large or 2 small (about 1.2kg) cauliflower
2 brown onions, halved and very thinly sliced
1½ slightly heaped teaspoons freshly ground cumin seeds
1½ slightly heaped teaspoons freshly ground coriander seeds
3 teaspoons sea salt flakes, or more to taste
½ teaspoon freshly ground black pepper, plus extra, to serve
¼ cup (60ml) extra-virgin olive oil, or more if needed
30g unsalted butter
3 large cloves garlic, finely chopped
2 small red chillies, finely chopped
400g potatoes, peeled and chopped into 3cm dice
1 teaspoon ground turmeric (or 2 heaped teaspoons finely chopped fresh turmeric)
1¼–1½ litres chicken (or vegetable) stock
1 tablespoon freshly squeezed lemon juice, or more to taste
plain yoghurt, to serve

Preheat your oven to 200°C. Line 1 large or 2 smaller baking trays with baking paper.

Cut the cauliflower (except for about 200g) into roughly equal-size 3–4cm florets. Tumble them into a large bowl with the onion, cumin, coriander, 1 teaspoon of the salt, and the pepper. Drizzle with 2 tablespoons of the olive oil and use your hands (wear prep gloves, if you like) to thoroughly mix everything together so the cauliflower is well coated in the spices. Spread the cauliflower mixture in a single layer on the prepared tray. Don't pile it up or the cauliflower will sweat rather than brown.

Roast the cauliflower for about 20 minutes, stirring once or twice, until it's speckled brown in patches and cooked through but with a little bit of bite.

Meanwhile, melt the butter in a large saucepan over low heat. Add the garlic and chilli and cook gently, stirring regularly, for 2–3 minutes (don't let the garlic brown or it will become bitter). Add the potato, turmeric and remaining salt, and swish them about to coat them in the buttery mixture. Pour in the stock, increase the heat to medium and bring the mixture to the boil. Reduce the heat to low so the mixture barely bubbles, cover the pan, and cook for about 20 minutes or until the potato is tender.

Scrape the cauliflower mixture into the saucepan. Once it returns to a gentle bubble, adjust the heat to maintain this and let it simmer for 5 minutes. Remove the pan from the heat and add 1 tablespoon of lemon juice. Use an immersion blender to puree the soup until it's smooth. Taste it and add more lemon juice and salt, if needed. If it seems a bit too thick, thin with a little more stock or water, but be careful you don't dilute the flavour too much.

Just before serving, use a very sharp knife to cut the reserved cauliflower florets into slices. Not all the slices will be perfect as the florets tend to crumble at their outer edges, but that's fine. Heat the remaining olive oil in a medium frying pan over medium heat and sauté the slices until they're speckled with gold. Remove the pan from the heat.

To serve, ladle the soup into bowls. Spoon a little yoghurt into each bowl, then top the soup with the sautéed cauliflower. Finish off with a good grinding of black pepper.

# Sweetcorn with smoked paprika butter and lime

Although our class days are long, I often find I wake early after them and lie quietly in bed listening to the dawn chorus of birds, smiling to myself as I think back over the past few days.

As much as I love teaching, one of the things I look forward to most in the build-up to our classes is the setting-up day. We arrive at the hall early, our car bursting at the seams with paraphernalia – baskets, boards, vases, cloths, and loads of produce and flowers. Our first job is to get the kitchen ready. Actually, that's not quite true, the very first thing we do is put the kettle on for an essential cup of tea! Next comes the hall and then my favourite part of all, doing the flowers and generally 'zhooshing' everything to make it shine. I feel just as I did when I was a little girl playing house. It's so much fun!

If possible, I always try to do one really unusual, food-related centrepiece for our morning tea table. This week it was a lovely old wire basket brimming with cobs of glossy black corn from my very clever farming friend and organic grower, Palisa Anderson. It seemed particularly appropriate, as one of the side dishes we were about to cook was freshly picked sweetcorn with smoked paprika butter, lime, chives and crème fraîche. I thought you might like to give it a try, as it's such an easy dish to make and goes exceptionally well with pretty much anything cooked on the barbecue. Also, it's just that little bit different. A word of advice, though, it's extremely more-ish, so you might like to double the recipe.

Happy Sunday. Belinda ♥

*We arrive at the hall early, our car bursting at the seams with paraphernalia – baskets, boards, vases, cloths and loads of produce and flowers.*

## Sweetcorn with smoked paprika butter and lime

SERVES 3–4 (AS A SIDE DISH)

2 cobs fresh sweetcorn
40g unsalted butter
1 small red chilli, finely
    chopped
1 teaspoon smoked paprika
1 teaspoon sea salt flakes
lime juice, to taste
1–2 tablespoons finely
    chopped chives, plus a little
    more, for garnishing
2–3 tablespoons crème
    fraîche, optional, to serve
freshly ground black pepper,
    to taste

These quantities are for two cobs of corn, which, depending on their size, serve three or four people as a side dish. Just double or treble the quantities for larger numbers.

Shuck the husks and silk from the corn cobs. Level the base, then stand the corn up and, steadying the top with your hand, use a large knife to carefully cut the kernels away from the core. Try to cut as close to the core as possible. Scoop the kernels into a bowl.

Melt the butter in a medium-size frying pan (use a large frying pan for bigger quantities) over medium-high heat. Add the chilli, smoked paprika and salt, and cook, stirring, for a couple of minutes to release the fragrance of the chilli and paprika.

Tip in the corn kernels and continue to cook, stirring regularly, for 6–10 minutes or until the corn is speckled brown and tender when you try a bit. Add a good squeeze of lime juice for a bit of a tang, taste it again and add more, if you like, then stir in the chives.

Scrape the corn into a shallow serving bowl and swirl in a dollop of crème fraîche, if using, and pepper to taste. Garnish with a smattering of extra chives.

*Sunday 21ˢᵗ June*

# Lemon curd and shortbread tart

We receive many comments about the beautiful rainbow eggs that we use in our cooking classes. I think virtually the first photo our students take when they arrive is of these eggs. Often, we'll find seven or eight different colours nestled within the one carton and it can take me a while to convince people that I haven't hand-painted them (see the eggs on page 4). We're trying to twist Obi and Ash's arms (of Good Goog Eggs) to do us a map, like the ones in chocolate boxes, so we know which eggs come from which one of their heritage chooks. We feel very fortunate to live just around the corner from their farm and even more so last week when Obi arrived at my front door, a big smile on his face and his arms laden with trays of the most gorgeous little eggs. He explained they call these 'practice' eggs, which are the first lays from their girls and, as they're too small to sell, he thought I might be able to use them. I think that's called an understatement!

Even though I've been using rainbow eggs for a long while now, I'm still blown away not only by their beauty, but also by the incredibly rich flavour and colour of the yolks – everything made with them looks as though it has been infused with saffron. As you can imagine, I've cooked up a storm of eggy things – lemon curd, lemon tart, chiffon cakes, ice-cream, let alone poached, boiled, scrambled and coddled eggs. This lovely lemon curd and shortbread tart is a particular favourite of mine. The shortbread 'pastry' is grated, so there's no rolling involved. And the lemon curd recipe isn't too sweet, which allows the tang of lemon to really come through. I hope you enjoy it!

Happy Sunday. Belinda 💜

*Often, we'll find seven or eight different coloured eggs nestled within one carton and it can take me a while to convince people that I haven't hand-painted them.*

# Lemon curd and shortbread tart

SERVES 8–12

icing sugar, for dusting
softly whipped cream or
    double cream, to serve,
    optional

**SHORTBREAD PASTRY**

2 cups (300g) plain flour,
    plus extra, for dusting
1 teaspoon baking powder
⅛ teaspoon salt
250g unsalted butter, at cool
    room temperature, roughly
    chopped
1 cup (220g) caster sugar
2 egg yolks (from 60g eggs)
2 teaspoons vanilla extract

**LEMON CURD**

3 × 60g eggs
90g caster sugar
½ cup (125ml) freshly
    squeezed lemon juice,
    strained
90g unsalted butter, melted
finely grated zest of 1 large
    lemon

The lemon curd in this tart is wonderful for all sorts of things, such as sandwiching cake or meringue layers, topping little pavlovas, folding into cream and plopping onto scones, or simply spreading thickly on toast. If you want to make a separate batch, it keeps well in the fridge for up to 10 days.

For the shortbread pastry, put the flour, baking powder and salt into the bowl of a food processor fitted with the steel blade and whiz them together so they're thoroughly mixed. Tip them into a bowl and set it aside.

Put the butter in the food processor along with the caster sugar and whiz for about 40 seconds or until the mixture is pale and creamy (you may need to stop the machine and scrape down the sides once or twice). Add the egg yolks and vanilla, then process again for 15 seconds or until well combined. Now add the flour mixture to the butter mixture and pulse the machine in short bursts until a ball of pastry forms around the blade (try not to overdo this mixing or the pastry may be a bit tough).

Turn the pastry out onto a board very lightly dusted with flour and shape it into 2 equal-size logs (if the pastry seems too soft, chill it for a little while so it firms up enough to handle comfortably). Wrap each log in baking paper, then pop them in the fridge and chill for at least 3 hours (or overnight) until they're really firm.

While the pastry is chilling, make the lemon curd. You can make the curd a week or so ahead, if you like. Put the eggs and caster sugar into a medium-size, heavy-based saucepan and whisk them together with a balloon whisk until they're thoroughly combined but not too frothy. Whisking gently, mix in the lemon juice and the melted butter.

Sit the pan over medium-low heat. Cook the mixture, stirring constantly with a flat-based wooden spoon or sauce whisk, until it thickens to a lovely, custard-like consistency. As you stir, try to use a figure-8 motion to cover the entire base of the pan so the curd doesn't catch and burn. The most important thing of all is not to let it boil, otherwise it may curdle. As soon as it's ready, remove the curd from the heat and strain it through a fine sieve into a heatproof jug. Stir in the lemon zest, then cover the jug loosely with a sheet of baking paper and leave the curd to cool. Once cool, cover securely and pop it into the fridge. It will keep well for up to 10 days.

Preheat your oven to 180°C. Very lightly butter a 25cm loose-based tart tin. Remove 1 pastry log from the fridge. Use the side of a box grater with the largest holes to grate the pastry onto a plate. I tend to do this in batches as the grater

fills quickly and the pastry strands will squash if they become too compacted. As you finish each batch, carefully transfer the grated dough to the prepared tin. When you have finished grating, gently pat the dough strands out evenly over the base of the tin, trying not to squash them down too much.

Now dollop the lemon curd evenly over the grated pastry. Smooth it out thinly with a palette knife as best you can, leaving a 1cm border around the edges. Grate the remaining pastry log the same way as before and sprinkle it over the lemon curd. Give it the lightest pat down to even it out.

Carefully transfer the tin to the oven (watch out you don't pop the base up – unfortunately, it's quite easily done) and bake the tart for about 35 minutes or until it's golden brown. Remove it from the oven and cool completely in the tin on a rack.

To serve, carefully remove the tart from the tin and place on a serving plate. Sometimes the tart may feel as though it's sticking to the tin and doesn't want to release from the base. If you find this happens, check underneath the tin to see if a bit of mixture has run out and stuck the base and sides of the tin together. If it has, use a fine palette knife to scrape away any crusted-on bits of pastry and the tart should release.

Dust the tart with icing sugar and serve with softly whipped cream. It's equally lovely served simply with a cup of tea or coffee or as dessert with double cream.

# Jalapeños with smoked pancetta and goat's cheese

After spending time away, the two things that ground me more than anything else are getting my hands in the soil in my garden (and today it won't be a minute too soon, as it's had a growth spurt in our mild winter and looks more like a jungle than a garden) and being in my kitchen once more. Despite a lifetime of cooking professionally, still one of my greatest joys is to potter about in the kitchen, washing vegetables, stirring pans, kneading dough for bread, and tasting little morsels of whatever I happen to be cooking. All the while in the background my mind hums along quietly suggesting what I could do with the ingredients in front of me. In a funny way it's a form of meditation, as my thoughts are so focused on what I'm doing that nothing else intrudes. This photo is of today's efforts, jalapeño peppers with goat's cheese and smoked pancetta. It's a riff on a dish we ate in Spain when we were able to visit my father-in-law last year before any of us had even *heard* the word 'Covid-19'.

Don't worry if the pancetta slides off the jalapeños as they cook; I just wiggle it back on again and also scrape any filling that may have leaked out back into the shells. They're rather gooey and most definitely a knife and fork job, but oh-so delicious! I'm very glad to say that my Number One tasting team – my husband, a dear friend, and my next-door neighbour (all three very good cooks and my severest and most honest critics) approved. So, I'm happy to report they'll be on next week's class menu.

Happy Sunday. Belinda

*I'm very happy to say that my star tasting team – my husband, a dear friend, and my neighbour (all three very good cooks and my severest and most honest critics) – approved.*

## Jalapeños with smoked pancetta and goat's cheese

MAKES 32

16 green jalapeño peppers
(choose ones with the stalks
still attached)
2 tablespoons extra-virgin
olive oil, plus more, if needed
¾ teaspoon sea salt flakes,
to sprinkle
360g marinated goat's cheese
(Persian or marinated feta is
good, too), drained
180g cream cheese, at room
temperature, chopped into
small pieces
32 small thin slices smoked
pancetta
freshly ground black pepper
good-quality crusty bread,
to serve

In Spain, these were made with jamón, however, with a wonderful local smallgoods maker, Salumi Australia, just over the hill from us, I used their smoked pancetta, instead. If anything, I think it's even better than jamón. Just so you know, jalapeños sit in the medium heat range for chillies; without the seeds and membranes they don't pack a big punch, but they can make your lips and tongue tingle. And one final thing, the cheese filling becomes quite molten as the jalapeños cook, so when we photographed these, I put about a teaspoon of fresh breadcrumbs into each jalapeño half before scooping the cheese on top – it did seem to absorb some of the filling and stop it becoming quite so runny.

Preheat your oven to 200°C. Line a shallow baking tray with baking paper and set it aside.

Halve the jalapeños lengthwise, then use a teaspoon to scoop out the seeds, core and any white membranes. As the halves are ready, drop them into a medium-size bowl. Drizzle over the olive oil and sprinkle with a little sea salt, then use your hands (I usually wear prep gloves for this as it's a bit oily) to toss the jalapeños until they're well coated. Once this is done, sit the halves, cut-side up, on the prepared tray.

Scoop the goat's cheese into a medium-size bowl and mash with a fork. Add the cream cheese to the bowl, then beat the cheeses together vigorously until the mixture is smooth. If you like, you can also do this with a hand-held electric beater. Use a dessertspoon to divide the cheese mixture evenly between the jalapeño halves – they will be fairly full. Top each one with a slice of pancetta and finish with a good grinding of black pepper. Chill the jalapeños for 20 minutes. If you like, you can make these hours ahead of time and keep them in the fridge until you're ready to cook.

Pop the tray into the oven and cook the jalapeños for 15–20 minutes or until they've softened slightly, the cheese is molten and the pancetta is just tinged with gold. Be careful not to let them cook for too long or they'll collapse and the cheese will run out. They'll still be delicious, but not quite as pretty as they should be.

Carefully transfer them to a platter and serve immediately with good bread to mop up the delectable oily juices.

# JULY

Smoky carrot and almond dip

Moroccan orange and almond syrup cake
with cardamom yoghurt cream

Slow-cooked star anise beef

Blueberry and blackberry crostata

*Sunday 5th July*

# Smoky carrot and almond dip

It's funny, but no matter how busy our cooking school days are and no matter how convinced I am that I'll sleep like a top after them, the adrenalin that keeps me going through the classes continues to kick in. Like our resident magpie with its early morning warbling of all it has heard during the day, I find myself bright-eyed and bushy-tailed at the crack of dawn, sifting and sorting through all that occurred.

So here I am, tucked up in bed, looking through what photos I managed to take of the classes: rows of lemon curd and the chilli and tomato jam that I made to go in the goodie bags (I have to say, I'm particularly chuffed about the latter, as I used our own homegrown tomatoes, which for the first time ever, have thrived this year); some of the baking we did – raspberry hand pies (see recipe, page 46), hazelnut crumble (see recipe, page 34), and crusty rye bread; a basket of flowers from a dear friend's garden; a berry compote made from the biggest, fattest, juiciest blueberries and mulberries I've ever eaten; and this addictive smoky carrot and almond dip to smear on bread.

As I look through the images, I find myself smiling, as each photo immediately conjures up a snatch of conversation, an exchange of ideas, the happy look on someone's face as they bake their first loaf of bread, that precious 'aha!' moment when something clicks about a technique or dish that has proved elusive. This is what I love about these photos – the memories of the many lovely people that we meet along the way. It makes all we do so very worthwhile.

Enough photo-gazing for now, I'm off to make a much-needed cup of tea and to join my magpie mate on the deck as he continues his gentle warbling, and I, my quiet pleasure in his song.

Happy Sunday. Belinda ♥

*I find myself bright-eyed and bushy-tailed at the crack of dawn, sifting and sorting through all that occurred.*

# Smoky carrot and almond dip

MAKES ABOUT 3 CUPS

70g whole blanched almonds
1kg carrots, trimmed and
    peeled
2 tablespoons extra-virgin
    olive oil, plus extra ½ cup
    (125ml), and more for
    drizzling
2 teaspoons sea salt flakes,
    or more to taste
1 small clove garlic, finely
    chopped
½–1 small chilli, finely chopped,
    optional
½ cup (90g) chickpeas,
    canned and drained
    or freshly cooked
1 tablespoon lemon juice,
    or more to taste
½ teaspoon freshly ground
    black pepper
¾ teaspoon smoked Spanish
    paprika
2 teaspoons roasted flaked
    almonds, to garnish
small herb leaves,
    to garnish, optional

This delicious vegan dip proved to be a big hit in the class – it makes a lovely change from hummus.

Preheat your oven to 180°C. Line 2 baking trays, 1 small and 1 large, with baking paper.

Spread the almonds on the smaller baking tray and roast them, stirring once or twice, for 6–8 minutes or until they smell nutty. Set them aside to cool, then coarsely chop.

Slice any thick carrots in half lengthwise, then slice all the carrots into 1½cm pieces or rounds. Tumble them into a large bowl and toss them with the 2 tablespoons of olive oil and 1 teaspoon of the sea salt. Spread them out in a single layer on the large baking tray, then pop them in the oven. Roast, stirring once or twice, for about 45 minutes or until they're very tender and starting to colour (don't let them get too dark as you want to retain their vivid colour). Remove the carrots from the oven and let them cool slightly.

Scrape the carrots into a food processor fitted with the steel blade (you can do this in a blender if you have a powerful one). Add the remaining 1 teaspoon of sea salt, garlic, chilli, chickpeas, lemon juice, pepper, smoked paprika, the extra ½ cup (125ml) olive oil and chopped almonds. Process, adding a little more oil if needed, until the mixture is smooth-ish. You can vary the texture to suit you, either coarse and chunky with almonds, or somewhat smoother. Taste the dip and add more oil, salt or lemon juice, if desired.

Pile the dip into a serving bowl, scatter with the roasted flaked almonds, drizzle with a bit more olive oil, and garnish with herb leaves. Any leftover dip keeps well in the fridge in an airtight container for up to 1 week.

*Sunday 12th July*

# Moroccan orange and almond syrup cake with cardamom yoghurt cream

Because of what I do, I realise that often people imagine I must have a very flash kitchen, but funnily enough, nothing could be further from the truth. It's small (there's a strict two-person limit or we constantly bump into each other!); there's not nearly enough bench space – so little in fact that I sometimes set up a trestle table in the dining area to take the overflow; I only have one oven (how I long for two); and it's not particularly sleek, as it's full of all sorts of bits and pieces that I treasure. But somehow it works and I'm very happy in it.

I think what brought this home to me was taking a photograph of a cake I'd just turned out onto my favourite wonky wire rack, which was given to me by a dear friend. It's things like this I love the most – the stuff of memories. My mum's bread knife; an old sieve with a faded red handle, a gift from Rodney, the photographer I've worked with for so many years (and who shot this book); the very first knife I ever owned, which is still razor-sharp and sits in a rack with its newer, sleeker contemporaries – all wonderful workhorses; some old, soft French linen tea towels my sister sent me; and the tin used for the cake in this photo – it occasionally sticks a bit, but that's more due to me not buttering it properly than to the tin itself. It was given to me by someone very special and any cake baked in it reminds me of her and, I'd have to say, takes on a certain chichi-ness, too!

Happy Sunday. Belinda 💜

*I realise that often people imagine I must have a very flash kitchen, but funnily enough, nothing could be further from the truth.*

## Moroccan orange and almond syrup cake with cardamom yoghurt cream

SERVES 16

2 cups (300g) plain flour
3 teaspoons baking powder
1 teaspoon freshly ground
    cardamom seeds, removed
    from pods* (or ready-ground
    cardamom)
½ teaspoon salt
⅔ cup (80g) almond meal
380g unsalted butter, at room
    temperature
380g caster sugar
6 × 60g eggs, at room
    temperature
finely grated zest of 2 oranges
100ml freshly squeezed
    orange juice
50ml extra-virgin olive oil
icing sugar, for dusting,
    optional

### ORANGE SYRUP
finely shredded zest
    of 3 oranges
1½ cups (375ml) freshly
    squeezed orange juice
finely shredded zest
    of 1 large lemon
¼ cup (60ml) freshly squeezed
    lemon juice
200g caster sugar
½–1 cinnamon stick
1 vanilla bean, split lengthwise
seeds from 6 cardamom pods*
4 oranges (preferably navels),
    peeled and segmented
cardamom yoghurt cream
    (see recipe, page 34),
    optional

Preheat your oven to 170°C. Butter a 25cm fluted Bundt tin and dust the tin with flour. (You can also bake the cake in a 26cm springform tin, but if you do this, line the base with baking paper.) Just a word of warning here, the lovely tin I use has such distinct ridges, that I find it best to butter the tin, chill it, then butter it again before flouring, so it's really well coated, otherwise the cake can stick in the ridges.

Put the flour, baking powder, ground cardamom seeds, salt, and almond meal in a large bowl and whisk them together with a balloon whisk for 1 minute. Set it aside.

Put the butter and sugar in the bowl of an electric mixer with the paddle beater and beat on medium speed for 4–5 minutes or until the mixture is light and creamy. Add the eggs, one at a time, beating really well after each addition. Scrape in the orange zest with the last egg.

Combine the orange juice and olive oil in a jug. Using a spatula, fold ⅓ of the flour mixture into the egg mixture, then fold in ⅓ of the orange juice and olive oil mixture. Continue alternating the flour and orange juice mixtures until all combined. Scrape the batter into the prepared tin (it will nearly reach the brim) and gently even the surface with the spatula. It's a good idea to make a very small depression with the spatula around middle of the batter to help the cake rise evenly.

Pop the cake in the oven and bake for about 1 hour and 10 minutes or until the centre springs back when lightly pressed. Sit the tin on a wire rack and leave the cake to settle for 15 minutes, then turn it out onto the rack. Once it's completely cool, rest another rack on top of the cake and invert the cake onto this. Now sit a large flat serving plate (or a gorgeous cake stand) on the base of the cake and invert the cake, one last time, onto this so it's right-side up.

While the cake is cooling, make the orange syrup. Put the orange zest, orange juice, lemon zest, lemon juice, sugar, cinnamon stick, vanilla bean and cardamom seeds into a medium–large saucepan over medium heat. Stir to dissolve the sugar, then stop stirring and bring the syrup to the boil. Reduce the heat so it bubbles steadily for 3 minutes, then turn off the heat and set the mixture aside to allow the flavours to infuse. Taste the syrup regularly and when the spice flavours are as you like them, strain the syrup through a fine sieve into a jug. (If you like, you can hang onto a little of the strained zest for decorating the top of the cake just before serving.)

Pour ⅓ of the orange syrup into a medium-size bowl. Add the orange segments and gently stir together, then cover the bowl and pop it into the fridge.

With a fine metal skewer, carefully pierce lots of deep holes all over the surface of the cake. Brush the remaining syrup evenly over the cake, allowing each lot to be absorbed before brushing on the next. Leave the cake to settle and the flavours to develop for 1–2 hours.

To serve the cake, use a paper towel or damp cloth to clean up any crumbs on the plate, then dust the cake with icing sugar or decorate with shreds of zest, if you've reserved them. Serve it with the orange segments in syrup, and the cardamom cream, if using.

* Removing the dark seeds from cardamom pods can be a bit fiddly, but fortunately the seeds themselves are becoming more widely available, so do keep an eye out for them. I prefer to grind cardamom seeds for the freshest, most aromatic flavour but you can also use ready-ground cardamom.

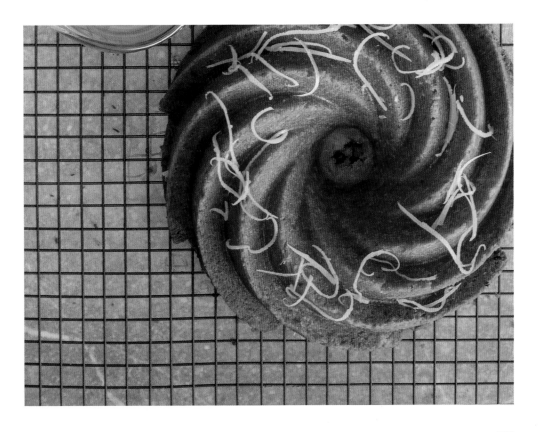

# Slow-cooked star anise beef

**With a side order of python!**

I've been sitting quietly writing at our dining table this morning, looking out on the lightening sky and the antics of the birds as they begin their day foraging through the callistemons outside the window. I love sitting here, as the birds are only an arm's length away and I can clearly see their exquisite markings. I can also hear their calls and, rather excitingly (if you haven't realised already, I'm a bit of a bird tragic), the fluting trills of that most elusive of birds, the scarlet honeyeater. More like The Scarlet Pimpernel, if you ask me. Every time I try to catch a glimpse, all I see is a blur of red and black as they swoop past! It's such a beautiful start to a day, and one I treasure.

We often eat our breakfast here, looking out on the passing parade of avian life. However, it's not breakfasts I'm talking about this morning, but dinner. Even here in the subtropics, we've had a few really cold nights and I know icy winds and snow are blasting much of the south, so I thought a recipe for a good, warming, slow-cooked stew might be in order. This particular one with its star anise, ginger, sticky dark soy sauce and fruity-sour tamarind flavours is always a winner. It takes a bit of time to prepare, but once everything is done, it's left to bubble gently in the oven for hours, filling the house with the warm fragrance of spice. Like all spiced dishes, it tastes even better after a day or two when the flavours of the spices have melded and mellowed into a more complex whole. We invariably split it into two or three batches, eating one lot immediately (the fragrance is too mouth-watering to resist), and squirreling away the other batches into the freezer.

*It takes a bit of time to prepare, but once everything is done, it's just left to bubble gently in the oven for hours, filling the kitchen with the warm fragrance of spices.*

Python alert! Meet our latest resident, a three-metre-long carpet python. He has been around for years, but recently has taken to stretching out in the sun on our deck. I can't tell you the surprise we had the other day when we were eating our lunch gazing out at the view, only to look down to find him gliding gracefully under the table between us. We must be getting used to him, as we both just lifted our feet and kept on eating our sandwiches!

Happy Sunday. Belinda 💜

# Slow-cooked
# star anise beef

SERVES 10

½ cup (125ml) light olive oil
4 onions, peeled, halved and
    thinly sliced
8 cloves garlic, finely chopped
½ cup finely chopped
    fresh ginger
3 teaspoons sea salt flakes
2 teaspoons freshly ground
    black pepper
1 teaspoon freshly ground
    cardamom seeds, removed
    from pods* (or ready-ground
    cardamom)
1 teaspoon ground cinnamon
1 teaspoon freshly grated
    nutmeg
½ teaspoon ground allspice
3 whole star anise
2kg chuck steak, cut into
    4–5cm pieces
1 cup (250ml) kechap manis
    (or dark soy sauce,
    at a pinch)
⅓ cup (90g) palm sugar
    (or dark brown sugar)
2 teaspoons tamarind
    concentrate dissolved in
    ⅓ cup (80ml) boiling water
tarragon or other herb leaves,
    to garnish
cooked jasmine rice and
    steamed greens, to serve

Just so you know, this isn't the most beautiful-looking dish, but it more than makes up for that with its wonderful flavour. It only needs a bowl of jasmine rice and steamed greens to round it out. By the way, if you like meat on the bone, this is wonderful made with beef short ribs but, of course, you don't get as many servings.

Pour half the oil into a large flameproof casserole dish (enamelled cast iron is perfect – mine holds just over 4 litres) and sit it over medium heat. When the oil is hot, add the onion and cook, stirring regularly, for 15 minutes or until it has softened and coloured a little. Add the garlic and ginger and cook for another 5 minutes. Stir in the salt, pepper, cardamom, cinnamon, nutmeg, allspice and star anise, and cook, stirring constantly, for a couple of minutes or until the spices have released their fragrance. Remove the dish from the heat and scrape the onion mixture into a bowl.

Return the casserole dish to the heat and pour in the remaining oil. Once it's hot, add a single layer of beef to the pan and fry to seal all over. When it's ready, scoop into a bowl and continue to cook the remaining beef in batches. If the pan starts to look a little dry, add a splash more oil.

While the beef is cooking, combine the kechap manis, sugar, and tamarind concentrate with its liquid in a large, heatproof bowl or jug. Pour in 1 litre of boiling water and stir everything together until well combined and the sugar has dissolved.

Preheat your oven to 150°C. Spread some of the onion mixture over the last batch of beef in the casserole dish, then spoon over more beef, followed by some onion. Continue to layer the beef and onion until they're all used up, then pour the kechap manis mixture over the top (this fills my casserole dish nearly to the brim). Return the casserole to the cooktop over medium heat. Once it starts to bubble, lay a sheet of baking paper on the surface, tucking it in around the edges, then cover with a lid. Transfer the casserole to the oven and cook for 3½ hours or until the beef is very tender.

When it's ready, let it settle for 10 minutes or so before serving. Depending on how well-trimmed the meat is, there will most likely be a layer of fat on the surface; use paper towel to blot it up. I like to take the casserole dish to the table and serve this family-style, but you can just ladle it straight into warm bowls on top of the rice (you'll need plenty of rice to soak up the savoury juices). Top with tarragon or herb leaves and serve with jasmine rice and steamed greens.

* Removing the dark seeds from cardamom pods can be a bit fiddly, but fortunately the seeds themselves are becoming more widely available, so do keep an eye out for them.

*Sunday 26th July*

# Blueberry and blackberry crostata

Just as well you don't have the ability to see the author of this post. As I write, I'm curled up on the sofa in my pyjamas with a thick pair of Clive's woolly socks on my feet, a rug tucked almost to the tip of my nose, and my neck swathed in a scarf – all I need is a beanie to complete things. All this swaddling is for good reason, though, as overnight the temperature plummeted and the air is as cold and keen as a knife this morning. I'm even wearing mittens! Still, a hot cup of tea and bowl of porridge with blueberries should help me thaw.

Speaking of blueberries, I have to confess I've nearly eaten my bodyweight in them these past few weeks as our local blueberry season is in full swing. We're able to buy seconds by the bucket from the farmers market and, needless to say, I'm using them every which-way at present. Apart from scooping handfuls from the bucket and eating them as is, they've found their way into all sorts of puddings, cakes and pies. I also made this simple blueberry and blackberry crostata for lunch with friends during the week. As I made it, I was thinking how crostatas really are my favourite dessert of all, they tick every box.

*I have to confess that I've nearly eaten my bodyweight in blueberries these past few weeks.*

- Short, buttery pastry

- Versatile, as they can be made with whatever fruit is in season

- Not too rich or sweet

- Easy to make and bake

- Utterly delicious!

If you've not made one before, do give this recipe a try as it really is very simple and you can use it as a template to mix and match fruit according to the season. In winter, a barely warm spicy apple or pear crostata is a joy, while in summer, peaches, plums and apricots come into their own. I hope you like it!

Happy Sunday. Belinda

# Blueberry and blackberry crostata

SERVES 8-10

### SHORTCRUST PASTRY

1½ cups (225g) plain flour
¼ teaspoon salt
125g unsalted butter, chopped
  into small pieces, chilled

### FILLING

4 large amaretti biscuits
  (or Dutch speculaas biscuits)
1½ tablespoons plain flour
1 heaped teaspoon ground
  cinnamon
¼ cup (55g) caster sugar
300g blueberries
300g blackberries
2 teaspoons white sugar,
  for sprinkling
blueberry or mixed berry jam,
  warmed (so it's a little runny)
double cream or vanilla
  ice-cream, to serve

Although you could use other biscuits in the filling (I've used both almond macaroons and digestives if I've been stuck), I find that the slightly bitter almond flavour of amaretti biscuits or the spicy goodness of Dutch speculaas biscuits are spot-on with stone fruits in particular. On that note, if you can, try to use fruit that is just-ripe and sweet, but not too soft or it may collapse a bit too much as it cooks (it will still taste wonderful, though). I've used both blueberries and blackberries in equal quantities here, but you can also just use blueberries, if you prefer.

For the pastry, put the flour and salt into a food processor fitted with the steel blade and whiz them together. Add the butter and process until the mixture resembles coarse breadcrumbs. With the motor running, steadily pour ¼ cup (60ml) iced water into the flour mixture. Continue to whiz until the dough forms a ball around the blade. Take it out, knead it gently just to bring it together and flatten into a disc. Wrap it tightly in cling film and chill for about 40 minutes or until it's firm but supple enough to roll. (If you've made the pastry 1–2 days ahead of time and kept it in the fridge, just remember that you need to let it soften a bit at room temperature, so it's supple enough to roll easily.)

Preheat your oven to 205°C. Line the base of a large, roughly 30cm-round pizza pan (or you can use a baking tray) with a sheet of baking paper and set it aside.

For the filling, put the biscuits in a ziplock bag and finely crush them with a rolling pin. Mix them with the flour, cinnamon and 2 tablespoons of the caster sugar (or whiz them all together in the food processor). Set this aside.

When the pastry is ready, roll it out to a thin round a bit larger than the prepared pizza tin. You need the pastry to be bigger than the tin, as this excess pastry eventually forms a border for the crostata. Drape the pastry over the tin, leaving an overhang all around and press it very gently into the sides. Spread the amaretti mixture evenly over the base, then sit the berries on top in a tightly packed layer. Sprinkle the berries with the remaining 1 tablespoon of caster sugar. Gently fold the pastry border over the fruit, pleating and pressing it gently to form a border of pastry. Sprinkle the white sugar over the pastry.

However, if you're making the crostata on a baking tray, once the pastry is rolled, centre it on the baking paper. Sprinkle the amaretti mixture evenly over the pastry leaving a 5–6cm border all around, so you can flip this over to form the rim of the crostata, then just continue with the recipe.

Bake the crostata for 35–40 minutes or until the pastry is crisp and deep golden brown. Remove it from the oven to a wire rack and leave it to cool in the tin for at least 40 minutes for the filling to firm up. After the crostata has cooled for 5 minutes, gently brush the warm jam over the berries, then continue to cool for the remaining 35 minutes. I can't tell you just how wonderful the crostata smells at this stage, but it's worth hanging on to eat it as its flavour really is best at room temperature when the juices have had a chance to meld with the biscuits.

With the help of the baking paper underneath, gently slide the crostata out of the pan and onto a large, flat serving plate. Serve with double cream or vanilla ice-cream.

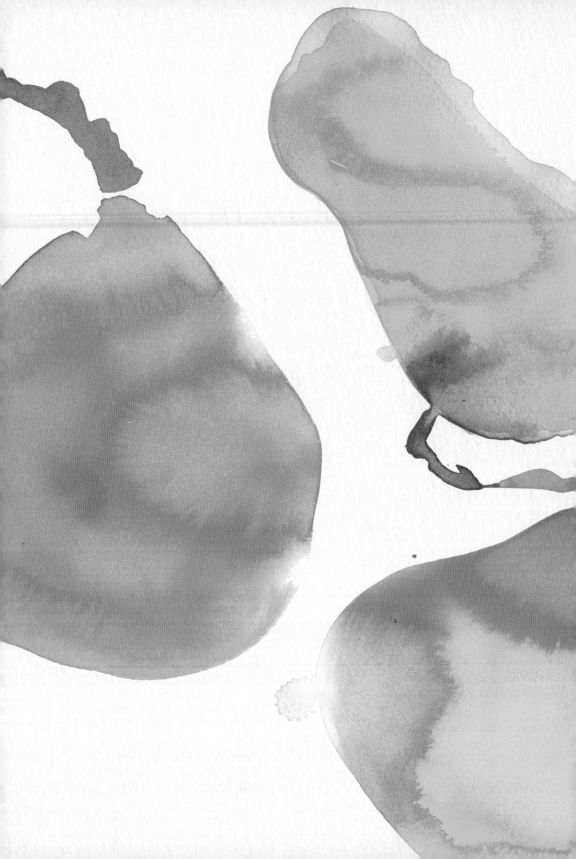

# AUGUST

Roasted pumpkin with hummus, yoghurt and pepitas

Hazelnut and apple upside-down cake

Caramelised fennel

Roasted lemon and chilli mushrooms

Orange, ricotta and honey tart

*Sunday 2$^{nd}$ August*

# Roasted pumpkin with hummus, yoghurt and pepitas

Talk about not seeing the wood for the trees! I made a rather lovely discovery a few weeks ago; unbeknown to me, a pumpkin vine had flourished in a pile of compost in a far-flung corner of the garden. As I cleared away some weeds, I spied three very substantial pumpkins nestled under their lush leaves, so I picked them and have let them harden in the sun. Tonight, we'll cut the first one and have it in a dish that has quickly become a family (and class, for that matter) favourite. It's a combination of spice-roasted pumpkin topped with crunchy pepitas and sesame seeds, and is accompanied by a cooling dollop of hummus and yoghurt. There are a few elements to the dish – the hummus, pumpkin and topping, but as they can all be prepared well ahead – the pumpkin coated and ready to roast; the pepitas waiting to be cooked; and the hummus made days before – it's straightforward to bring together.

I find it goes beautifully with Middle Eastern dishes and looks really vibrant if you scatter pomegranate seeds over the top. But it's also fantastic for jazzing up a simple meal – chicken, fish, or sizzling lamb chops straight off the barbecue; roast chook fragrant with garlic and lemon; or even a meal of spicy lentils and rice. All so very good!

Happy Sunday. Belinda 🌱

*I made a rather lovely discovery a few weeks ago; unbeknown to me, a pumpkin vine had flourished in a pile of compost in a far-flung corner of the garden.*

## Roasted pumpkin with hummus, yoghurt and pepitas

SERVES 6

¾ cup (180ml) my tried-and-true hummus (see recipe, page 52)
1½ medium-size (about 1.4kg trimmed weight) butternut pumpkins (or use a mixture of pumpkins, such as Kent, marron and butternut)
100ml extra-virgin olive oil
2 teaspoons freshly ground cumin seeds
1½ teaspoons sea salt flakes, or more to taste
¾ cup (210g) thick Greek-style yoghurt
pomegranate seeds, to garnish, optional

#### PEPITA, SESAME AND CUMIN TOPPING
1½ tablespoons (30ml) extra-virgin olive oil
40g pepitas
2 slightly heaped teaspoons sesame seeds
20g unsalted butter
¾ teaspoon freshly ground cumin seeds (or sumac)
½ teaspoon sea salt flakes

Just a couple of things before you begin, the hummus recipe makes considerably more than you need for this dish, but I always make the full quantity as we love it, and I find it really useful to have tucked away in the fridge. Secondly, the pepitas add a lovely crunchy finish to the dish, but they do tend to jump out of the pan as they cook, so you need to be careful not to be splattered with them. If you'd rather, you can just toss the pepitas and sesame seeds in the olive oil, spread them on a baking tray lined with baking paper and roast in a 180°C oven until the sesame seeds are golden and the pepitas 'pop' and become light and crunchy. Then simply tip them into a bowl and swirl in the butter, ground cumin and sea salt.

Make sure the hummus is made before you start the pumpkin. Preheat your oven to 220°C. Line 1 large or 2 smaller shallow baking trays with baking paper and set them aside.

Cut the butternut pumpkin in half lengthwise. Use a large spoon to scoop out and discard the seeds. It's up to you whether you peel the pumpkin or not. I like the skin on, but make sure the skin is well washed and dried if you do this. Slice the pumpkin crosswise into 2cm-thick slices. Depending on the size of the pumpkin, you may need to halve these if it's really large. (If you're using Kent pumpkins, I find these look best cut into wedges.)

Sit the pumpkin slices in a bowl, drizzle them with the olive oil and sprinkle with the cumin and salt. Use your hands to thoroughly mix them together so the pumpkin is well-coated. Spread the pumpkin in a single layer on the prepared tray or trays, then pop in the oven to roast for about 40 minutes, turning the pieces halfway through the cooking time, so they become tender and dark brown in patches.

Meanwhile, stir together the yoghurt and hummus. Taste the mixture and add a bit more of each, if necessary, and salt to taste. Scrape the mixture into a serving bowl, cover it tightly and set it aside in a cool spot. This keeps well in the fridge for at least 5 days.

Just before the pumpkin is ready, make the pepita, sesame and cumin topping. Heat the olive oil in a small frying pan over medium heat. Add the pepitas and sesame seeds and cook, stirring constantly, until they're golden. Just be careful when you do this as the pepitas will pop like crazy, so if you have one, use a splash guard or lid, otherwise protect your hands and arms with oven gloves. Take the pan off the heat and swirl in the butter, cumin and sea salt.

Remove the pumpkin from the oven. You can serve it straightaway or let the pumpkin cool to room temperature.

To serve, dollop a little of the hummus mixture over the base of a serving platter. Sit the pumpkin slices on top, then dollop over more of the hummus mixture. Spoon the pepita, sesame and cumin topping over, then sprinkle with pomegranate seeds, if using. Scoop any remaining hummus and yoghurt mixture into a bowl and serve it alongside.

**P.S.** The beautiful orange-skinned pumpkins in the photograph are a variety called marron (the French word for chestnut), so named because the flesh has a rich chestnut flavour.

*Sunday 9<sup>th</sup> August*

# Hazelnut and apple
# upside-down cake

During the week as I was slicing apples for a cake, I popped a morsel into my mouth and, within a moment of taking that first crisp bite, I was hurtled back in time to my childhood. I was standing in our garden with my sister, eating sharp little Jonathan apples and competing to see who could spit the pips the furthest. Much to Mum's chagrin, these spitting competitions continued throughout the year, the only variable being the pips we used – they changed according to the season. Apples, mandarins, grapes and watermelon all took their turn (and on one memorable occasion, the polished, black seeds of custard apples, as my dad loved the fruit and would buy them by the tray). But watermelon seeds were our favourite, because they were quick to germinate and downy little watermelon vines would pop up all over the garden. I don't think Mum was too impressed that her garden was being colonised by watermelons! Nor could she quite believe that her two daughters delighted in doing this. Although, we were such tomboys that it can't have come as too much of a surprise.

I do so love the way a scent, a fleeting glimpse of someone, a piece of music and, in this case, the taste of something, can transport us to a particular place in time. It's funny, though, it wouldn't have happened with just any old apple, it was those particular, slightly astringent little apples I was using for the cake that did it. On a far more practical note, those little apples made a mean cake, too, and that cake is the glossy upside-down one you see here. It's such a winner!

Happy Sunday. Belinda ♥

*Much to Mum's chagrin, these spitting competitions continued throughout the year, the only variable being the pips we used – they changed according to the season.*

# Hazelnut and apple upside-down cake

SERVES 10–12

135g hazelnuts, roasted and
　skins rubbed off
1 cup (150g) plain flour
1 teaspoon salt
1 teaspoon bicarbonate
　of soda
½ teaspoon baking powder
1½ teaspoons ground
　cinnamon
1 teaspoon mixed spice
¼ teaspoon freshly grated
　nutmeg
1–2 apples (about 200g),
　peeled, cored and chopped
　into 1cm dice
120g unsalted butter, at room
　temperature
½ cup (110g) caster sugar
¼ cup (55g) packed brown
　sugar
2 × 70g eggs at room
　temperature and lightly
　beaten
1½ teaspoons vanilla extract
½ cup (125ml) buttermilk
maple syrup, for brushing,
　optional
crème fraîche, double cream
　or vanilla ice-cream,
　to serve

## TOPPING
30g unsalted butter
600g small apples (pink lady
　or royal gala), peeled,
　halved and cored
¼ cup (55g) packed brown
　sugar

You will need a 25cm (or thereabouts) ovenproof,
non-stick frying pan to make this lovely, spicy apple
cake. Sweet apples, such as pink lady or royal gala, are
particularly good in this recipe as they keep their shape
when they cook. Small apples are also ideal, but if you
can only find larger ones, you'll need to quarter rather
than halve them. The finished cake won't look quite as
pretty, but it will still taste every bit as wonderful. By
the way, this is delicious served with the salted caramel
sauce on page 170.

Preheat your oven to 180°C. For the topping, add the butter
to a 25cm ovenproof, non-stick frying pan, then sit the pan
over medium heat. Once the butter has melted, swirl the
pan to coat the base and sides with butter, then remove it
from the heat.

Arrange the apple halves, cut-side down, in a single layer
over the base of the pan. Return the pan to the heat. Cook the
apples, undisturbed, rotating the pan over the heat so they
cook evenly, for 5–10 minutes (depending on how juicy they
are) or until they're golden brown. Carefully turn the apples
over and cook for another 5 minutes or until a knife slides
through them with a hint of resistance. Transfer the apples
to a plate, cut-side up, and leave them to cool a little.

Return the pan to the heat and add the brown sugar
and 1 tablespoon of water. Stir with a wooden or silicone
spoon until the sugar has dissolved. Stop stirring and let
the mixture cook, swirling the pan once or twice, for up to
1 minute or until it's thick and bubbling in a thin layer over
the base of the pan. Remove the pan from the heat and let the
caramel mixture cool a little. Arrange the apple halves, cut-
side down and evenly spaced, over the top. Set aside.

Meanwhile, tip the hazelnuts, flour, salt, bicarbonate of
soda, baking powder, and spices into the bowl of the food
processor fitted with the steel blade. Whiz them together
until the hazelnuts are fairly finely ground. It doesn't matter
if there is a mixture of big and little pieces of hazelnut. Tip
all except 1 tablespoon of the mixture into a bowl and set it
aside. Sprinkle the reserved tablespoon of hazelnut mixture
over the diced apple, toss to coat and set that aside, too.

Add the butter, caster sugar and brown sugar to the
bowl of the food processor and whiz until pale and creamy-
looking. With the motor running, pour in the beaten egg and
vanilla and whiz, stopping to scrape down the sides of the
processor once or twice, until the mixture is soft and creamy.
Tip in half the hazelnut mixture and pulse to combine. Pour
in the buttermilk and pulse briefly to incorporate it, then add
the remaining hazelnut mixture and pulse to just combine.

Remove the lid from the processor and stir in the reserved diced apples. Dollop the batter over the apples in the pan, then use a palette knife to spread it as evenly as possible, pressing down gently to work it into the spaces between the apple halves.

Place the cake in the oven and bake for 35–40 minutes or until the top is brown and the cake springs back in the middle when gently pressed. Carefully transfer the pan to a rack and let it cool for 10 minutes. Gently run a small palette knife around the sides of the pan to loosen the cake. Sit a serving plate or cake stand over the top of the pan and, using oven gloves to protect your hands, grasp both the pan and plate and flip them over to release the cake. Carefully remove the pan. If any apple or cake sticks to the pan, scrape them off and gently press them back onto the cake.

To serve, brush a little maple syrup over the top to give the apples a sheen. Serve warm or at room temperature with crème fraîche, double cream, or, best of all, vanilla ice-cream.

**P.S.** Although the cake looks best on the day it's made, it does keep for a couple of days in an airtight container at cool room temperature. It also freezes remarkably well for up to a month; just warm it gently before serving.

*Sunday 16ᵗʰ August*

# Caramelised fennel

Although our classes on the weekend were the last for winter, they felt like an ode to spring. We filled the kitchen and hall with the most beautiful, fragrant flowers. Jonquils jostled with paper daisies; our olive tubs overflowed with grevilleas and wax flowers; tendrils of jasmine wound their way down the dining table; sweet peas scented the air; and exquisite little flowers from the organic flower farm just down the hill were the most perfect simple finish to our desserts. But it wasn't only the flowers that reflected the change in season, the ingredients did, too. Slender bulbs of green garlic went into pies; meaty red peppers and tomatoes became a vibrant soup; paper-thin slices of fennel mellowed in olive oil; and intoxicatingly fragrant passionfruit flavoured our morning tea muffins.

I can't begin to tell you the pleasure it gives me to share this bounty from our local farms (and the gardens of generous friends) with our students. It's what inspires me every day and why I love what I do. It was so lovely yesterday, when even in all the hustle and bustle of a busy class, I took a moment to step back, look around and just enjoy the delight and pleasure on the faces of our students as they, too, revelled in it all.

Perhaps my favourite recipe in the class was the most unprepossessing in many ways – a simple side dish of sautéed fennel and carrots. It doesn't have many ingredients, but the flavours are true and clear and the warm, rounded anise fragrance of the fennel shines through. It was a hit with everyone. I hope you like it.

Happy Sunday. Belinda 💜

*Although our classes on the weekend were the last for winter, they felt like an ode to spring.*

# Caramelised fennel

SERVES 4 (AS A SIDE DISH)

3 large fennel bulbs
60g unsalted butter
⅓ cup (80ml) extra-virgin
    olive oil
2 medium-size onions, halved
    and finely sliced
2 medium-size carrots, peeled
    and thinly sliced into rounds
1 cup (250ml) good, rich
    chicken stock (preferably
    homemade)
2 bay leaves
2 teaspoons sea salt flakes,
    or more to taste
lemon juice, to taste

If you're lucky enough to get fennel that still has its leafy fronds, cut them off pretty much level with the top of the bulbs, but reserve some of the delicate leaves for garnishing. Now trim the bases flat, and check the outside layers of the bulbs – if they're really coarse or badly bruised, peel them away and discard them. Halve each bulb lengthwise, make a V-shaped cut to remove the central core, then slice the halves thinly.

Add the butter and oil to a very large frying pan (or use 2 smaller frying pans and divide the oil and butter evenly between them). Sit the pan over medium heat. When the butter and oil are hot, scrape the onion and carrot into the pan. Cook, stirring regularly, for about 8 minutes or until the onion is golden. Add the fennel to the pan and cook, stirring regularly, for about 15 minutes or until it's partly golden. Pour in the chicken stock and add the bay leaves along with the sea salt.

Now, cover the pan. If you don't have a lid that fits, sit a baking tray on top, but just be careful to use oven gloves or a thick tea towel to remove it, as it can get very hot. Cook the fennel for another 20 minutes or so, giving it a good stir every so often, until it's meltingly tender and golden brown. If it doesn't look golden enough, increase the heat slightly and cook until it does. Add a good squeeze of lemon juice, then taste the fennel and add more lemon juice or salt, if needed.

Using a slotted spoon, transfer the fennel to a serving dish. If there's more than about ⅓ cup (80ml) of liquid left in the pan, return the pan to the heat and boil off the excess. Taste it, and when it's as you like it, pour it over the fennel mixture.

You can pretty much eat this at any temperature – hot, barely warm (my favourite, as I think it does the flavours the most justice) or cool. It keeps well for at least 5 days in a sealed container in the fridge.

# Roasted lemon and chilli mushrooms

One of the main reasons I decided to hold my cooking classes close to home is due to the astounding array of produce that grows here. Much has changed since we arrived 19 years ago and what was a trickle of locally grown produce has now become a veritable flood. It has been wonderful to see the farmers markets flourish and to count so many local growers and food artisans as our friends. I feel an intense joy when I look around the kitchen during a class and see baskets and buckets overflowing with fruit, vegetables and flowers, all grown close by, more often than not by people we know. And always, in some small way, there is an offering from our own garden, too. Perhaps a jug of society garlic flowers, a posy of herbs, or lemons from our trees. It gives me a feeling of great contentment and it's what informs the dishes we cook.

Last weekend's class was no exception. There were candy-coloured dahlias from the nearby flower farm; fragrant waterlilies; masses of oranges, lemons and limes as citrus season is well underway; searingly hot scotch bonnet chillies and wonky little green capsicums (an unexpected gift from a lovely woman who had walked past the kitchen door and seen us cooking); a plethora of mushrooms; the sweetest, milkiest corn; beautiful eggs; and tea and coffee grown just up the road. It really does fill my heart that I'm able to share all this with our participants. The dishes we cook are simple so they highlight the flavours of the bounty we have to work with. It's such fun! I hope you have a really gentle day.

Happy Sunday. Belinda 🖤

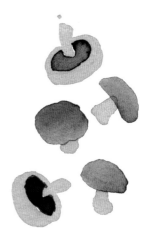

*Always, in some small way, there is an offering from our own garden, too – a jug of society garlic flowers, a posy of herbs, or lemons from our trees.*

## Roasted lemon and chilli mushrooms

SERVES 6

270ml extra-virgin olive oil
6 cloves garlic, crushed
2 small eschalots (or 1 large),
   peeled and roughly
   chopped (or use 2 sliced
   spring onions)
3 small red chillies, 1 halved
   lengthwise, 2 finely chopped
¼ cup thyme leaves
finely grated zest of 1½ lemons
1½ teaspoons sea salt flakes,
   plus extra, for sprinkling
900g mushrooms, sliced into
   fat wedges
freshly ground black pepper
thyme sprigs, to garnish

I've made this recipe with all sorts of mushrooms and it works well with any variety. Just choose the freshest mushrooms you can find.

Pour the oil into a small saucepan, then add the garlic, eschalot, and halved red chilli. Sit the pan over medium–low heat and bring to just below the boil so it bubbles very gently. Remove the pan from the heat and stir in the thyme leaves, lemon zest and salt. Cover the pan with a lid and leave the oil mixture to infuse for at least 20 minutes or up to 1 hour.

Preheat your oven to 220°C. Line a large-ish baking tray with baking paper.

Use an immersion blender or regular blender to puree the oil mixture. Strain it through a fine sieve into a jug, making sure you press down on the solids with the back of a spoon to extract as much oil as possible. Discard the solids.

Tip the mushrooms into a large bowl. Trickle the flavoured oil over the top, then use your hands to thoroughly mix the mushrooms and oil together so the mushrooms are glistening. Scrape the mixture onto the prepared baking tray and spread out in a single layer.

Roast the mushrooms, stirring a couple of times, for about 20 minutes or until tender and golden brown. Remove the tray from the oven, sprinkle the chopped chilli over the top, then tumble the mushrooms into a serving dish. Sprinkle it with a little more sea salt, grind over some black pepper and garnish with thyme sprigs.

# Orange, ricotta and honey tart

I've just slipped back into bed with a cup of tea while the rest of the house sleeps. As I write, I can hear the gentle coo of bar-shouldered doves outside the window as they forage about on our deck in the hope of finding a little seed. I love the sound of their soft calls to each other, and I suspect those calls are for me, too, as I have no doubt they're somewhat impatiently waiting for me to finish my tea to put out breakfast for them. But first, I have some planning to do.

We have family staying and a birthday dinner to prepare for tonight, so I'm busy making a mental list of what needs doing. There's focaccia dough to make; eggplants to be charred; tables to set; and all the myriad other jobs, both big and small, that go into making a special meal. And then, of course, there's the most important thing of all – the birthday cake (or in this case, birthday tart). I'm still tossing up about this one – the birthday girl adores pastry and I'm very tempted to make a tart as the 'cake', but then again, I would hate her to be disappointed that it wasn't a proper birthday cake. Although, that said, considering she seeks out pastry desserts wherever she is in the world and has quite possibly eaten more sweet tarts than anyone I've ever known, I probably shouldn't give it another thought! Except to get out of bed and get started. I hope that today is a happy and peaceful one for you.

Happy Sunday. Belinda ♥

*I've just slipped back to bed with a cup of tea while the rest of the house sleeps and, as I write, I can hear the gentle coo of bar-shouldered doves outside the window.*

# Orange, ricotta and honey tart

SERVES 8–10

1 blind-baked simple
   shortcrust pastry tart shell
   (see recipe, page 84) made
   in a deep 25–26cm
   loose-based tart tin
icing sugar, for dusting
softly whipped cream,
   to serve, optional

## FILLING
450g ricotta*
250g neufchâtel**, quark
   (or cream cheese)
½ cup (110g) caster sugar
1½ tablespoons clear honey
4 × 60g eggs
1 cup (250ml) pure cream
finely grated zest of 1 orange
1 teaspoon vanilla extract
1 tablespoon Grand Marnier
   (or another orange liqueur)

This really is a lovely tart. The ricotta filling is delicate and light with a haunting orange flavour and the pastry gives just the right amount of crisp contrast. I think it's best served barely warm, but if you would rather make it ahead, you can chill it and return it to room temperature before serving – the texture will be just a little denser if you do this. It's wonderful served with poached or roasted fruit – quinces, rhubarb, and plums are all terrific with it.

Preheat your oven to 170°C. Sit the tart tin with the shell on a baking tray and set it aside.

For the filling, put the ricotta and neufchâtel into the bowl of a food processor fitted with the steel blade and whiz them together until smooth. Add the caster sugar and honey and, with the motor going, add the eggs, one at a time, stopping and scraping down the sides occasionally. Add the cream, orange zest, vanilla and liqueur and whiz them together until the mixture is smooth.

Scrape the mixture into the prepared tart shell, then carefully transfer the tray with the tin to the oven. Bake the tart on the lowest shelf in the oven for about 45 minutes or until the top is golden and the filling begins to crack and appears set up to 5cm in from the edge. It should be a little wobbly, but still feel set. The best way to test this is to lightly place your hand on the middle of the tart and give it a gentle jiggle – it will wobble like panna cotta. Transfer to a wire rack and leave it to cool until it's just-warm or at room temperature.

Gently slip the tart out of its tin onto a serving plate, dust lightly with icing sugar and serve with whipped cream.

 * The best ricotta to use for this is the kind that has been drained in a sieve. Many supermarkets sell ricotta in little tubs, but it has additives in it and isn't nearly as delicious in the tart.

** Neufchâtel is similar to cream cheese, but is ever so slightly tangier and has a lower fat content.

# SEPTEMBER

Tomato tarte Tatin

Cucumber salad with yoghurt dressing and crunchy buckwheat

Salted caramel sauce

Fabulous chicken mayonnaise sandwiches

Homemade mayonnaise

## Sunday 6th September
# Tomato tarte Tatin

At Friday's farmers market it felt as though summer had arrived, rather too early, but it was lovely nonetheless. Although there were still cauliflowers, broad beans and beautiful greens in abundance, my eyes were drawn to trays of basil seedlings, colourful little red and yellow Roma tomatoes, beautiful crimson peppers, and strawberries so fragrant I could smell them three stalls away. As ever, my good intentions not to buy too much flew out the window and by the time we left my trolley was groaning under the weight of it all.

So, it was home to unpack our booty and I'm happy to report that much has been put to good use already. Three jars of the most luscious strawberry jam have been added to my pantry (still my all-time favourite with homemade scones), I'll plant the basil seedlings this afternoon, and the tomatoes are destined for a recipe that has been buzzing round my mind for a while, a tomato tarte Tatin.

When I'm working on a recipe, it's wonderful if all goes well first-time round, but that's often not necessarily the case. I find I go back to it again and again, tweaking something here, changing a quantity there, adding something new – it can take an inordinate amount of time. But I do love it and it's incredibly satisfying when all the pieces of the puzzle fall into place. Although, I should hasten to add that not everything works out and I've abandoned more recipes than I care to think about! However, I'm pleased to say that this tart is a real winner. It's intensely tomato-y and surprisingly light – so much so, that the two of us demolished most of it on our own! It never ceases to delight me just how many wonderful dishes can be created from a handful of ingredients. I hope you enjoy it, too.

Happy Sunday. Belinda 💜

*It never ceases to delight me just how many wonderful dishes can be created from a handful of ingredients.*

# Tomato tarte Tatin

SERVES 3–4

## PASTRY

1 cup (150g) plain flour
pinch of salt
85g cold unsalted butter,
    chopped into small pieces

## THE TOMATOES

600g (about 16) smallish
    Roma tomatoes
40g unsalted butter
2 tablespoons extra-virgin
    olive oil
1 large clove garlic, finely
    chopped
1–2 small red chillies, finely
    chopped
2 teaspoons caster sugar
¾ teaspoon sea salt flakes,
    or more to taste
freshly ground black pepper,
    to taste
1½ teaspoons balsamic
    (or fig) vinegar
basil leaves, to garnish,
    optional

Gorgeous as this tart looks, it's actually very simple to make, however, you do need a good 24cm non-stick, ovenproof frying pan to make it – ideally one with straight, rather than sloping sides. If you like, you can make the pastry a few weeks ahead and freeze it, then just defrost it in the fridge overnight.

For the pastry, whiz the flour and salt together in a food processor. Add the butter and whiz everything again until the mixture resembles medium breadcrumbs. With the motor running, pour in 2 tablespoons (40ml) iced water and process only until the dough forms a ball around the blade. The time for this varies a bit depending on the weather, when it's warm it seems to come together faster.

Tip the dough out onto a board and shape it into a ball. Now, flatten it into a disc and wrap it tightly in cling film. Chill the disc in the fridge for 30–40 minutes or until the pastry is firm but supple enough to roll out. By the way, if you want to make the pastry ahead of time, it keeps well in the fridge for up to 3 days, but it will be too firm to roll at this stage, so let it warm to room temperature until it's pliable.

Line a large baking sheet with baking paper. Roll the pastry out on a lightly floured board into a roughly 4mm-thick round, just slightly larger than the diameter of your 24cm frying pan. Using a dinner plate of similar size to the frying pan as a guide, cut a round slightly larger than the diameter of the frying pan. Pick the pastry up on your rolling pin and unfurl it onto the lined baking sheet, then pop it in the fridge while you prepare the tomatoes.

Preheat your oven to 200°C. Line a large plate or baking tray with paper towel.

Halve the tomatoes lengthwise and use a teaspoon to scoop out and discard the seeds and pulp. Sit them on the prepared tray, cut-side down, to drain. After 15 minutes, pat them dry.

Melt half the butter with half the oil in the frying pan over medium-low heat. Remove the pan from the heat and sit the tomatoes, skin-side down, in the pan. Make sure they're tightly packed and slightly overlapping so they completely cover the base of the pan (if necessary, add a couple of extra tomato halves). Dot the rest of the butter on top and drizzle with the remaining oil. Sprinkle the garlic, chilli, sugar, salt, pepper and vinegar evenly over the top. Return the pan to the heat, and cook the tomatoes for 5–8 minutes or until the bottoms are colouring up (the juices will bubble around them). Turn the pan regularly as you do this, so the tomatoes caramelise evenly. As soon as they're ready, turn off the heat.

While the tomatoes are cooking, take the pastry round out of the fridge. When the tomatoes are ready, working quickly as the pastry softens rapidly, gently press the pastry round on top and tuck it down the sides of the pan. Cut 3 × 3cm slits in the top of the pastry to allow steam to escape. Now just pop the pan into the oven and bake the tart for 25–30 minutes or until the pastry is golden and crisp. If you notice the pastry is puffing up during the first 15 minutes or so of baking, carefully press it down again (I slip my hand into a silicon oven glove to do this).

A word of warning, you need to be really careful and use thick oven gloves or thick tea towels when you do this next step as the handle will be red-hot. When the tart is ready, take it out of the oven and leave it to settle for a few minutes. Then sit a large, flat serving plate or board on top of the pan and invert the tart onto it. If any bits of tomato stick to the pan, just ease them off and press them back on the tart. Garnish with a few basil leaves and eat it straightaway.

*Sunday 13<sup>th</sup> September*

# Cucumber salad with yoghurt dressing and crunchy buckwheat

As I write this, I have a packet of frozen peas wrapped around my left knee and I can't help but smile wryly to myself, as I suspect only a cook could sustain an injury from a very large chunk of parmesan cheese. This particular chunk fell out of the fridge and somehow found the one tender, unprotected spot on a human being's knee to land! Within minutes of cheese and knee colliding, a lump the size of an egg swelled up and, this morning, after a few days of standing teaching, it has come back to haunt me.

On an entirely different note, my obsession with cucumber salads continues apace, as this is the time of year when the sweet and ever so cucumber-ish, finger-length Lebanese cucumbers arrive in the market. Their flesh is crisp and dense and I find myself using them every which-way. So far, we've had pickled cucumbers heady with dill and coriander seeds; Asian cucumber salad, fragrant with lime and chillies; and thinly sliced cucumbers and radishes mounded over labne to be scooped into warm, puffy pita bread – so delicious! This particular salad is on repeat at the moment. It came about when I was teaching at Rodney and Severine Dunn's beautiful The Agrarian Kitchen Cooking School in Tasmania. Rodney is a brilliant chef and whipped up a cucumber salad for us to have with lunch – it has stayed in my mind ever since. This is my take on that memorable dish. It's a modest salad in some ways, but is addictively crisp and refreshing and such a lovely foil to spicy dishes.

I had best say goodbye as the peas are melting fast and I need to hunt down some more!

Happy Sunday. Belinda 🖤

*Only a cook could sustain an injury from a very large chunk of parmesan cheese.*

# Cucumber salad with yoghurt dressing and crunchy buckwheat

SERVES 4–6

1kg small Lebanese
   cucumbers, peeled and
   halved lengthwise
1 tablespoon extra-virgin
   olive oil
2 tablespoons buckwheat
   groats
¼ teaspoon sea salt flakes

**YOGHURT DRESSING**
1 cup (280g) thick Greek-style
   yoghurt
1 dessertspoon tahini
1 small clove garlic, very finely
   chopped, or more to taste
1 teaspoon sea salt flakes,
   or more to taste
½ teaspoon freshly ground
   cumin seeds
freshly ground black pepper,
   to taste
50ml extra-virgin olive oil
1 tablespoon finely chopped
   chives, optional

For this salad, the smaller the cucumbers the better, as they're the sweetest. The buckwheat topping only takes a couple of minutes to make and is great to have in your repertoire as it adds the most satisfying crunch to all sorts of salads.

For the yoghurt dressing, put the yoghurt, tahini, garlic, salt, cumin and pepper into a bowl and mix them together. Trickle in the olive oil, whisking all the while so the mixture is homogenised. Taste the mixture and add more salt if needed, then cover the bowl and pop it into the fridge. Just prior to serving, stir in the chopped chives, if desired.

With the tip of a small teaspoon, carefully scoop out the seeds from the cucumber and discard. Slice the cucumber halves diagonally into 3cm pieces, then tumble them into a bowl and chill them.

Just before serving the salad, heat the olive oil in a small frying pan over medium heat. Add the buckwheat groats and cook, shaking and turning the pan constantly, for 2–3 minutes or until they're darker and tinged with gold. Remove the pan from the heat and tip the buckwheat into a small sieve sitting over a jug to catch the oil. As soon as it has drained, tip the buckwheat into a small bowl and sprinkle with a little sea salt.

To serve, spoon about ⅓ of the cucumber salad into a serving bowl, then spoon a little dressing over the top. Repeat this twice more with the remaining cucumber and dressing, then sprinkle over the buckwheat.

# Salted caramel sauce

Let's talk caramel. I do so a lot in my classes for there is something quite magical about the ability of just one ingredient, sugar crystals, to be transformed into so many different guises.

Sprinkle those crystals into a good, heavy-based saucepan, melt them over high heat and the most extraordinary alchemy takes place – they transform from solid crystals to a glossy, dark liquid caramel, which has a remarkable range of uses. Carefully add cream, vanilla and sea salt, swirl it back over the heat and you have the best salted caramel sauce ever; mix in a handful of chopped nuts, coffee beans or shreds of citrus zest, pour it onto a baking sheet lined with baking paper and it will set solid again to make the most beautiful, sparkling praline; swirl the liquid caramel around a cake tin, add custard and gently cook in a water bath and you have one of the world's classic desserts, crème caramel. Simpler still, add a soupçon of orange juice, then pour it over peeled oranges and let them sit for an hour or so until the juice and caramel meld into a brilliant sauce. But it's not just sweet dishes that benefit from this transformation, add fish sauce, lime juice, chillies and ginger and you end up with a wonderful glaze for chicken or prawns. There is just so much you can do with it.

However, there are three golden rules to keep in mind when you caramelise the sugar:

*Let's talk caramel. There is something quite magical about the ability of just one ingredient, sugar crystals, to be transformed into so many different guises.*

1.  Wash any crystals off the sides of the pan as the sugar caramelises to help prevent it candying and becoming cloudy.

2.  It can give you an awful burn, so be very careful when you're handling the pan.

3.  And lastly, be brave and take it to the point where it's darker than you feel it should be and has a whiff of a burnt edge. It's this contrast of sweet yet slightly bitter that makes it such a sensational ingredient.

Happy Sunday. Belinda ♥

# Salted caramel sauce

MAKES ABOUT 1½ CUPS (375ML)

1 cup (220g) caster sugar
¾ cup (180ml) pure cream
1 teaspoon vanilla extract
1 teaspoon sea salt flakes

This sauce keeps well for at least six weeks in the fridge and can be used for all manner of delicious things. It's divine poured over vanilla ice-cream or spooned onto a steamed pudding, and takes the already wonderful hazelnut and apple upside-down cake on page 144 to a whole new level. It's also a fabulous accompaniment to a simple chocolate cake or brownie, transforming them from a morning or afternoon treat to a special dessert.

Pour the sugar and ½ cup (125ml) water into a heavy-based saucepan over medium heat. Stir until the sugar dissolves, then stop stirring, increase the heat to high and bring the mixture to the boil. Allow it to boil, undisturbed, washing down the sides occasionally with a brush dipped in water to remove any sugar crystals that may form. Once the syrup turns a light amber colour, watch it like a hawk. You want it to become a gorgeous, rich brown, but not so dark that it burns. When it's ready, remove the pan from the heat and pour in the cream. Be mindful to protect your hands with long oven gloves or thick tea towels when you do this, as the caramel may well spit and bubble up. Return the pan to gentle heat and stir to dissolve the caramel into the cream. Finally, swirl in the vanilla extract and salt, then set the pan aside. Once the sauce is cool, pour it into a jar, seal it tightly and store it in the fridge for up to 3 weeks. Return the sauce to cool room temperature before using.

*Sunday 27th September*

# Fabulous chicken mayonnaise sandwiches

I have to admit that one of my all-time favourite things to eat is a really good sandwich. I have a friend who feels the same way (and quite possibly makes the best egg sandwiches in the world). So when she came for lunch the other day, sandwiches, or one sandwich in particular, was on the menu, as we'd waxed lyrical about it a few weeks earlier – chicken mayonnaise. When they're good, they're truly great. So I thought this morning, I'd put down my 10 golden rules for making brilliant chicken sandwiches. They're actually a really useful thing to master with Christmas not too far away. If you make them from a square loaf, trim the crusts and cut them into fingers, they make the most delicious, substantial finger food to have with a festive drink – Champagne, preferably!

*My 10 golden rules for making brilliant chicken sandwiches.*

**The 10 golden rules**

- The bread must be fresh and just a little robust – a good sourdough loaf makes for a terrific sandwich.

- The chicken should be top-quality and gently cooked so it's moist and full of flavour.

- The bread must be generously buttered right to the edges. I do mean butter here, margarine doesn't cut it at all, ever!

- Ideally, the mayonnaise should be homemade (see recipe, page 175). Honestly, it only takes about 10 minutes to make a batch by hand (and would take half that time if you make it in a blender).

- The filling must be moist and have a little bit of crunch – very finely sliced celery is perfect, about ½ cup to 1 whole chicken is ideal.

- It also needs bite – a couple of tablespoons of chopped chives should do the trick.

- Salt is essential, be liberal with it.

- It should be plump with filling, there's nothing more depressing than a mean sandwich.

- A few rocket leaves add a lovely bit of punch and colour.

- Be sure to make plenty of them as they'll disappear like hotcakes!

## Fabulous chicken mayonnaise sandwiches

MAKES 24–27 FINGER
SANDWICHES OR
8 REGULAR ONES

1 × 1.6kg organic or free-range
    chicken
3 spring onions, chopped
2 stalks celery, chopped
parsley stalks, optional
1 cup (250ml) homemade
    mayonnaise (see recipe,
    opposite page) or good
    store-bought mayonnaise
2–3 teaspoons sea salt flakes
freshly ground black pepper,
    to taste
½ cup very finely sliced celery
¼ cup finely chopped flat-leaf
    parsley
2 tablespoons finely chopped
    chives
16–18 slices good-quality
    wholegrain, wholemeal or
    robust white sourdough
    bread (if you want to make
    finger sandwiches, use a
    rectangular loaf)
softened butter, for spreading
a big handful of rocket leaves,
    optional
a handful of flat-leaf parsley
    leaves, to garnish

If you want to make the sandwiches ahead of time, store them in a sealed container in the fridge with baking paper on the bottom and between each layer. They'll keep well for at least 4–5 hours; just return to cool room temperature before serving.

Choose a saucepan large enough to completely submerge the chicken. Add about 3½ litres water, the spring onion, celery and parsley stalks and bring to the boil over high heat.

Lower the chicken into the pan, breast-side down, and let the liquid return to the boil, then reduce the heat to low so that just a few bubbles rise steadily to the surface. Leave the chicken to cook, uncovered, for 40 minutes, skimming off any froth that floats to the top. You'll find the chicken tends to bob to the surface, so what I do is sit a heatproof plate on top to ensure it stays submerged. Turn off the heat, cover the pan tightly and leave the chicken to steep in the liquid for another 15 minutes.

Gently lift the chicken out of the stock, being extra careful not to tear the skin, and allow any liquid to drain from the cavity. The easiest way to do this is by inserting the handle of a wooden spoon through the cavity of the chicken, so you can scoop it out of the pan without damaging the skin. Funnily enough, although the skin is later discarded, it's important to keep it intact because the chicken forms a jelly-like layer between the skin and the flesh as it cools, which helps keep it moist. Immediately plunge the chicken into a deep bowl (or saucepan if you don't have a deep enough bowl) of iced water so that it's completely submerged. Leave the chicken to cool in the water for 1 hour. This plunge into iced water will give the chicken a wonderful moist, juicy texture. Reserve the chicken stock for another use.

Drain the chicken, discard the skin (although I tend to keep a little skin, as I like it in the filling). Remove the meat from the bones, then tear or chop it into small pieces (add the skin at this point, if you're using it) and put it into a bowl. Stir in the mayonnaise, salt, pepper, celery, parsley and chives, then taste it and adjust the flavour to suit you.

Lay the bread slices out in front of you and spread each slice generously with butter. Put a thick, even layer of the chicken mixture onto half the slices, spreading it right to the edges. Sit a few rocket leaves, if you're using them, on top of the chicken filling and sandwich with the remaining bread. If they're just for us for lunch, I slice them in half and sit them on a platter. However, if you're making finger sandwiches, the process is a little different. Trim off the crusts, then cut each sandwich into 3 fingers. Line them up in rows on a long platter and sprinkle some parsley leaves over the top to garnish.

# Homemade mayonnaise

MAKES ABOUT 320ML

2 egg yolks (from 60g eggs),
    at room temperature
½ teaspoon Dijon mustard
½–⅔ cup (125ml–160ml)
    extra-virgin olive oil
½ cup (125ml) olive oil
2 teaspoons white wine
    vinegar or freshly squeezed
    lemon juice, or more to taste
¾ teaspoon sea salt flakes,
    or more to taste

A little tip before you begin, sometimes, when I've been hurrying too much, I've added the oil too quickly and the mayonnaise has split. If this should happen to you, I've found that immediately adding a little lemon juice and a splash of hot water can quite often salvage it. However, it may need more of each than the recipes states, in which case you'll need to adjust the final texture and flavour.

Sit a medium-size bowl on a damp cloth (this will help stop the bowl sliding around) and plop the egg yolks and Dijon mustard into it. Whisk together with a balloon whisk until they're thoroughly mixed. Now, combine both oils in a jug.

This next stage of proceedings is the only slightly tricky thing about making mayonnaise. The secret to it is patience, because if the oil is added too rapidly the mixture will separate. Whisking constantly, start adding the oil, drop by drop. As the mixture starts to come together and thicken you can increase the flow of oil to a very fine thread. The mixture should become really thick and glossy. About halfway through adding the oil, add the vinegar or lemon juice and ½ tablespoon of very hot water or more as necessary – this will thin the mayonnaise a little and make it easier to mix. Continue adding the remaining oil in a fine stream until it is all incorporated – add another ½ tablespoon of very hot water as you go. Whisk in the salt, then taste the mayonnaise and add a little more vinegar, lemon juice or salt to suit your taste.

If speed is of the essence, you can easily make the mayonnaise in a blender, or food processor. Put the egg yolks and mustard into a blender, and whiz to combine. Then, much like the process of making it by hand, slowly trickle in the oil with the blender going. As it starts to thicken, add  the vinegar or lemon juice and ½ tablespoon of very hot water or more as necessary. You can add the oil at a faster rate than when you make it by hand, but still be careful as it can curdle. Finish off in the same way as handmade mayonnaise.

If you're not using the mayonnaise straightaway, scrape it into a container with a tight-fitting lid and pop it in the fridge, where it keeps well for up to 4 days.

# OCTOBER

Burrata with roasted tomato and capsicum

A delicate asparagus tart

Black garlic butter

Almond, coconut and raspberry cake

*Sunday 4th October*

# Burrata with roasted tomato and capsicum

I'm afraid I'm putting a bit of a spanner in the works by doing my regular Sunday morning post on Saturday evening, as I'm on an early flight to Sydney tomorrow to teach. The class isn't until Monday night, but with a full house and loads of prep to do, I need to be there well ahead of time.

I must admit, I have my fingers and toes crossed we don't have any hiccups en route, for my luggage is full of food. I always have a little smile to myself when I go away to teach, as invariably my suitcase has a small pile of clothes tucked into one corner while the majority of the space is taken up with all sorts of cooking paraphernalia – a set of knives; my favourite rolling pin (a very well-travelled rolling pin at that, as it has been a faithful companion at various cooking schools around the world); two Bundt cake tins; my much-loved, off-set palette knife; a battered old travelling teapot and leaf tea (two essentials that I can't survive without); and, more often than not, some of my favourite local ingredients in our hand luggage. In this case, they include the lightest, most delicate crème fraîche from my lovely friend and award-winning cheesemaker, Debra Allard; eight fat burrata and a kilogram each of smoked mozzarella and ricotta from The Byron Bay Mozzarella Company; a bucket of blueberries; bags full of beautiful little crimson and yellow Roma tomatoes; and a container of tiny lavender society garlic and chive flowers from my garden. Wish me luck that it all gets there intact!

The burrata are to be used in the following recipe. It's actually a dish I often make at Christmas time, as the creamy white burrata, deep-red capsicums and tomatoes, and bright-green basil leaves look so festive and beautiful. I hope you enjoy it!

Happy Sunday. Belinda 💜

*I must admit, I have my fingers and toes crossed that we don't have any hiccups en route, for my luggage is full of food.*

# Burrata with roasted tomato and capsicum

SERVES 6

550g (about 32 large) cherry
   or miniature Roma
   tomatoes, halved
extra-virgin olive oil,
   for drizzling
sea salt flakes, for sprinkling
caster sugar, for sprinkling
1 large clove garlic, very finely
   sliced
2 large red capsicums (look for
   ones that are evenly shaped)
balsamic or fig vinegar
a little of your favourite salad
   dressing (or see recipe,
   page 96), if needed
a small handful basil (or mint)
   leaves
3 burrata
freshly ground black pepper,
   optional

Miniature Roma tomatoes are ideal for this recipe, if you can get your hands on them. When serving, you'll need to put out a sharp knife and large serving spoon, so that your guests can cut into the burrata, then scoop its creamy centre and the tomato mixture onto their plates.

Preheat your oven to 150°C. Line a shallow baking tray with baking paper.

Sit the tomato, cut-side up, in the prepared tray. Drizzle over oil, then sprinkle a small pinch of salt and sugar onto each tomato half. Stir the garlic into a bit more olive oil and spoon it around the tomatoes. Pop the tray in the oven and roast for about 1 hour or until the tomato halves have shrunk somewhat and are a bit wrinkled. Leave them to cool to room temperature. (When I've been pushed for time, I've cooked the tomatoes in a hotter oven, about 180°C, for 30 minutes or so. They're not quite as luscious as the slow-cooked ones, but at a pinch, they're just fine.)

Meanwhile, slice the capsicums down their natural contour lines into large pieces. Remove the cores, seeds and white ribs and place, shiny-side up, on a grill or baking tray. Slide them under a preheated hot grill until the skins blister and blacken. Remove and cover with a thick tea towel. As soon as the capsicum is cool enough to handle, peel away the skins and slice into strips (you can do this up to a week ahead of time and store, covered with olive oil and a soupçon of vinegar, in the fridge). Scoop the capsicum into a bowl and add the tomatoes. Pour a good splash of balsamic or fig vinegar into any juices left from the tomatoes and drizzle this mixture over the top. Very gently mix them together. Taste the mixture and add more balsamic vinegar or salt, if needed. Pour on a little salad dressing if the juices look a bit meagre. Add most of the basil (or mint leaves) just before serving.

To serve, spoon the tomato mixture evenly down a rectangular platter. Make 3 small hollows in the mixture and sit a burrata in each one. Trickle the burrata with a little olive oil or salad dressing, and scatter the remaining basil (or mint leaves) over everything. Grind over some black pepper, if liked.

*Sunday 11<sup>th</sup> October*

# A delicate asparagus tart

How I love seeing the change of seasons reflected at the
farmers market. There was a notable shift this week from
the more robust greens and fruits of winter to the gentler
hues and more delicate flavours of spring. Broad beans
(so young their pods were velvety to touch) jostled with
finger-length zucchinis; the first bags of nectarines
appeared at Gary, the honey man's stall; bunches of
fragrant sweet peas lined up next to carrots the size and
shape of golf balls; and knobbly, heirloom tomatoes in
a rainbow of colours beckoned invitingly from the tomato
stall (needless to say, quite a few ended up in my trolley).
But perhaps the best treats I came away with were two
bunches of slender asparagus spears and a paper bag
brimming with tiny, freshly dug new potatoes. The perfect
springtime duo! The asparagus was gently cooked, then
slipped into a tart shell and topped with a delicate,
herb-flecked custard and dollops of soft, creamy feta.
The potatoes were scrubbed and steamed (not that they
needed much scrubbing, as the skins were so fine and
papery that they came away with the rub of a fingernail),
before being dressed with a knob of butter, a handful of
tiny mint leaves and a sprinkling of sea salt. The two were
such a lovely springtime combination – creamy, wonderfully
potato-y potatoes and the delicate, herb-strewn tart.

Happy Sunday. Belinda 🖤

*Broad beans (so young
their pods were velvety
to touch) jostled with
finger-length zucchinis,
and heirloom tomatoes
in a rainbow of colours
beckoned invitingly.*

# A delicate asparagus tart

SERVES 6–8

1 blind-baked simple
 shortcrust pastry tart shell
 (see recipe, page 84) made
 in a 25–26cm tin
350g asparagus spears
5 × 60g eggs
200g crème fraîche
 or sour cream
1 cup (250ml) milk
1 teaspoon sea salt flakes
freshly ground black pepper,
 to taste
about ⅛ teaspoon freshly
 ground nutmeg
1 heaped tablespoon finely
 chopped fresh tarragon
 (or chervil)
1 heaped tablespoon finely
 chopped flat-leaf parsley
1 heaped tablespoon finely
 chopped dill
2 heaped tablespoons
 chopped chives
200g soft, creamy feta or
 marinated goat's cheese,
 drained and lightly crushed
2 tablespoons finely grated
 parmesan
an assortment of herb sprigs
 and leaves, to garnish

My favourite cheese for this recipe is Meredith Dairy's marinated goat's cheese in extra-virgin olive oil with garlic and herbs. It's available in supermarkets and delis.

Preheat your oven to 175°C. Sit the tart tin with the pastry shell on a baking sheet and set it aside.

Cut off and discard the woody bases of the asparagus spears and peel them if the skins seem tough. When they're all done, slip the asparagus spears into a large frying pan of lightly salted, boiling water and adjust the heat so the water bubbles gently around them. Cook for about 3 minutes or until they're tender but still lovely and green (you may have to do these in batches if your pan is small). As soon as they're ready, drain the spears, then dunk them in a bowl of iced water to stop them cooking. Wrap them in a thick tea towel and gently pat dry, then slice the spears on the diagonal into bite-size pieces.

In a large bowl, lightly whisk the eggs with a balloon whisk to break them up. Add the crème fraîche (or sour cream), milk, salt, pepper and nutmeg, and whisk everything thoroughly together. Finally stir in the herbs. Pour the mixture into a jug, cover it and put it in the fridge until you're ready to use it – you can do this 1–2 hours ahead of when you need it.

When you're ready to bake the tart, scatter half the asparagus pieces evenly over the base of the pastry shell, then strew half the feta (or goat's cheese) over the top. Repeat this with the remaining asparagus and feta. Give the egg mixture another quick whisk as it will have settled somewhat, then pour it into the tart shell. I usually do this right by the oven, or put the baking sheet with the tart shell on the partly pulled-out oven shelf and then pour in the liquid as it's easy to spill if you carry the sheet any distance, which I've learned the hard way!

Slide the baking sheet with the tart carefully into the oven. Cook for 20 minutes, then sprinkle grated parmesan evenly over the top. Bake the tart for another 20 minutes or until the filling is still a little wobbly but set. The best way to check is to lightly rest the palm of your hand on the filling and give it a gentle jiggle.

Remove the tart from the oven and leave it to settle in the tin for 5 minutes or so (it's also lovely eaten at room temperature). To serve, slide the tart onto a serving platter and garnish with herb sprigs and leaves.

## Sunday 18ᵗʰ October
# Black garlic butter

As I write this, the house is redolent with the fragrance of crushed coriander and cumin seeds, cinnamon, allspice, the hot, sharp scent of beautiful little bird's eye chillies from the garden, and the wonderful, mellow fragrance of black garlic – the latter bought from our friends John and Lyndall Picone of Picone Exotics. As well as being a brilliant grower, John is a master cook and I wait patiently each year for his precious stock of black garlic to appear at their market stall. Basically, black garlic is regular garlic that has been heated over a long period of time so the sugars caramelise and darken. When you slice across the cloves, they look like black jelly and have a wonderful flavour – softer, deeper and more rounded than fresh garlic. I mainly use it to finish off a dish, as the flavour is somewhat ephemeral and can disappear if it's cooked for a while.

*As well as being a brilliant grower, John is a master cook and I wait patiently each year for his precious stock of black garlic to appear at his market stall.*

Apart from using it in salad dressings, I always top up my stock of black garlic butter with those first bulbs from John. It's so easy to make and is beyond delicious, adding a wonderful depth of flavour to all sorts of things. Try melting it onto chargrilled steaks or slices of barbecued eggplant; slather it onto homemade crostini and top with peppery salami; sauté mushrooms in olive oil and just before serving, swirl through a knob of black garlic butter; dollop it onto roasted carrots – the possibilities are endless.

To make it, simply beat 250g room temperature unsalted butter with a wooden spoon until it's soft and light. Scoop the jelly-like interior from 6–10 good-size black garlic cloves and add to the butter along with a sprinkling of sea salt. Beat with a wooden spoon until everything is well combined. Taste it and add more salt, if necessary. I occasionally add a smidgen of anchovy fillet to add another layer of flavour. Lay a sheet of foil on the bench and cover it with a sheet of baking paper. Scrape the butter onto the end of the baking paper nearest you and shape it into a 20cm-long log. If it's too soft, chill it briefly to firm it up. Roll the butter in the paper and foil, twisting both ends of the foil tightly in opposite directions to make a bon-bon. Refrigerate for at least 4 hours or until it's firm enough to slice. It freezes well for up to 5 weeks.

Happy Sunday. Belinda 🖤

# Almond, coconut and raspberry cake

Oh, what a week! You know that feeling when you start out a week with a plan (quite probably my first mistake) and everything starts to go pear-shaped from there? Well, this has been one of those weeks. There has been laughter and some tears, quiet moments and times of avid conversation, a fair bit of 'will we, won't we', and underpinning it all, there has been food. I often say to my husband that I think I was brought into this world to feed people, big and small, for my default position in both happy and challenging times is to head into the kitchen and cook. It grounds me in a way that nothing else can – I feel my shoulders drop, my focus sharpen, my thoughts settle, and then there is the quiet joy of sharing whatever it is that I've made with others. It always turns my world the right way up again. So, as you can imagine, there has been a flurry of kitchen activity these past few days.

*You know that feeling when you start out a week with a plan (quite probably my first mistake) and everything starts to go pear-shaped from there?*

I've experimented with cakes, made a completely inedible soup (truly, it was awful), baked bread, chopped chillies and tomatoes for relish, and even made pink-iced cupcakes at the request of my favourite 10-year-old. Successes and failures, just like life, really. Fortunately, out of it only good has come – a more peaceful heart and some new recipes to boot, two of which we ate for dinner last night. A gently spicy chicken noodle salad and a rather more-ish almond, coconut and raspberry cake. The salad still needs a bit more tweaking, but this slender cake, with its beautiful moist texture and delicate flavour, is a complete and utter winner and is going on the menu for my next cooking classes. Funny how life works out at times, isn't it?

I hope this coming week proves to be a kind and gentle one for you.

Happy Sunday. Belinda 💙

# Almond, coconut and raspberry cake

SERVES 8-10

250g unsalted butter
100g almond meal
50g desiccated coconut
70g plain flour
½ teaspoon baking powder
7 large (from 70g eggs)
   eggwhites, at room
   temperature
250g icing sugar mixture
½ teaspoon salt
1 teaspoon vanilla extract
icing sugar, for dusting
fresh or dried rose petals,
   to decorate, optional
softly whipped cream,
   crème fraîche or ice-cream,
   to serve

### RASPBERRY PUREE

150g fresh (or frozen)
   raspberries
60g caster sugar
12g cornflour

As you only need the eggwhites for this recipe, I usually make a batch of mayonnaise and custard with the leftover yolks. The cake keeps well for 2–3 days at room temperature and leftovers can be frozen for up to 5 weeks. To defrost, return to room temperature or warm gently before serving.

For the raspberry puree, put the raspberries and sugar into a small saucepan and gently mix them together. Leave them to sit for 15 minutes to help the raspberries release their juices.

Sprinkle the cornflour over the berries, then sit the pan over medium heat and bring the mixture to the boil, stirring regularly. Adjust the heat so it bubbles gently for 1 minute, frequently scraping the base of the pan with a spoon, until the mixture is thick and a little darker, then remove the pan from the heat. Pour the mixture into a heatproof bowl and allow it to cool without stirring. (If you stir at this stage you run the risk of the cornflour breaking down and the mixture becoming runny.) The raspberry puree can be used as soon as it's cool or can be kept in the fridge in a sealed container for up to 1 week, just return it to room temperature before using it.

Preheat your oven to 180°C. Butter a 23–24cm springform tin and line the base and sides with buttered baking paper.

Melt the butter in a medium saucepan over medium–low heat. Remove the pan from the heat and leave the butter to cool until it's lukewarm.

Tip the almond meal, coconut, flour and baking powder into a bowl and whisk them together with a balloon whisk for 1 minute or until they're thoroughly combined. Set the bowl aside.

Tip the eggwhites into a clean, dry mixing bowl and sift in the icing sugar mixture and salt, then use a hand-held electric beater on medium speed to combine the mixture until it's just smooth, but not foamy or fluffy. Add the almond mixture and beat briefly again until just combined. Finally, with the beaters going, pour in the cooled butter and vanilla, and mix until combined. The batter will be quite runny, which is as it should be. Scrape the batter into the prepared tin and spoon dollops of raspberry puree evenly over the top.

Bake the cake for 40–45 minutes or until the centre springs back slightly when gently pressed and a fine skewer inserted into the middle comes out clean. Let the cake cool in the tin for 10 minutes, then carefully remove the sides of the tin and rest a flat plate on top of the cake. Invert the cake onto this, then ease away the base and baking paper and carefully invert the cake again onto a wire rack. Leave it to cool completely.

To serve, carefully transfer the cake to a serving plate or cake stand, dust with icing sugar and scatter with rose petals. Serve with softly whipped cream, crème fraîche or ice-cream.

# NOVEMBER

Tortilla Española

Almond skordalia

A classic ginger cake

Goat's cheese labne with cucumber and radish salad

Fragrant spiced chicken with minted yoghurt

Dark chocolate, caramelised date and hazelnut brownies

# Tortilla Española with almond skordalia

The longer I cook, the simpler my cooking becomes. I relish the pure, clear flavours of the ingredients I'm using and much of what I try to do is draw them out rather than over-embellish them. This was brought home to me again yesterday, when for the umpteenth time, I made a tortilla Española, a Spanish omelette.

Many is the time I've eaten this in Spain, as my father-in-law lives there and it's one of the classic dishes offered as tapas when we go out for a drink. The best one I ever tasted was in a tiny seafront bar near where he lives in Nerja. We ordered our drinks and the first tapa to arrive was a plate of golden, deep-fried eggplant. It was completely plain except for a sprinkle of coarse salt and drizzle of sticky, dark cane syrup, and yet oh-so perfect. After another drink, a platter bearing a still-warm Spanish omelette was put in the centre of the table. To say we fell on it is an understatement; we virtually inhaled it and the plate, too!

*A platter bearing a still-warm, Spanish omelette was put in the centre of the table. To say we fell on it is an understatement!*

Ever since, I've tried to replicate it. Finally, yesterday, I came closer than I ever have before and realised, yet again, why it's one of Spain's most celebrated dishes. Soft, golden eggs bind meltingly tender chunks of potato imbued with the fragrance of the olive oil they're slowly cooked in. There's a hint of sweet, gently cooked onion, salt to add a little sharpness and, really, that's it. Five ingredients and heaven on a plate! With simple dishes like this, the devil is in the detail – it's all about technique. (I know it's gilding the lily just a little, but I often serve this with a bowl of garlicky almond skordalia to spoon on top of each serve – the two go so beautifully together).

Happy Sunday. Belinda 💜

# Tortilla Española

SERVES 4

300ml extra-virgin olive oil
1 large onion, quartered and
    very finely sliced
2 cloves garlic, peeled and
    lightly crushed
800g waxy potatoes (desiree,
    kipfler or Dutch cream),
    peeled and cut into
    1cm pieces
8 × 60g eggs
2 teaspoons sea salt flakes
small handful finely chopped
    flat-leaf parsley, optional,
    plus extra whole leaves,
    to serve
almond skordalia, to serve
    (see recipe, page 198)

As I've worked on this recipe, I've discovered a few ways of doing things that aren't necessarily traditional, but they certainly make a difference. I like to start the onion and garlic cooking slowly in the oil before adding the potato, so the oil becomes imbued with their fragrance. I have to say here, traditionalists will shudder at the thought of adding garlic, but I love the extra depth of flavour it gives. The addition of a little chopped parsley is definitely not usual, either. However, it really does add a rather lovely colour contrast to the golden eggs and potatoes. And (purists please look away) the other thing I sometimes do, is add a little chopped chilli and a few pinches of smoked paprika to the potatoes as they cook – it really does add a certain something to the dish, as do pieces of cooked chorizo stirred into the tortilla mixture.

Heat the oil in a 24cm non-stick frying pan over low heat. Add the onion and garlic and cook gently for about 8 minutes or until they start to soften and look translucent. Add the potato and cook, turning regularly, for 15–20 minutes or until it's tender with a golden tinge here and there. Adjust the heat so the oil bubbles steadily and evenly. You don't want the potato to colour very much or crisp, it just needs to cook through until tender. (I know this seems like a lot of oil, but the whole idea is not just to cook the potato but to flavour it with the oil. The excess oil is drained away at the end and can be reused to cook other savoury things or for your next tortilla.) When the potato is ready, gently slide the mixture into a large sieve over a bowl to allow the oil to drain away; reserve this excess oil. You can remove the garlic, if you like, but I leave it in as it's soft and tender.

Break the eggs into a large bowl and sprinkle with the salt. Use a fork to very gently break up the eggs a little. They should only need half-a-dozen whisks, they're not meant to be combined. Tip the hot potato mixture into the eggs and stir everything together. Set the bowl aside for 20–30 minutes to allow the potato to absorb a little of the egg and for the flavours to develop.

Wipe out the pan, add a couple of tablespoons of the reserved cooking oil and set it over medium heat. If you're using parsley in the tortilla, mix it into the egg mixture now, then pour the mixture into the pan and spread the potato out evenly. Stir with a fork for the first minute or so (not touching the base or sides of the pan), then leave the tortilla to cook for 1 minute, shaking the pan occasionally to prevent it sticking. Reduce the heat to low and cook for another 3–4 minutes or until it's set and golden underneath.

(Just be mindful that depending on the pan you're using and the heat underneath it, the cooking times will vary quite a lot, so you'll need to use your judgement.) It's a good idea to rotate the pan over the heat every so often, so the base heats evenly. Check the sides of the tortilla by carefully easing them back from the edge of the pan with a palette knife or spatula. Once they look set and golden, but the surface of the tortilla is still rather wet, it's time to turn it over. (Please see Plan B, below, if this all seems a bit too daunting.)

It takes a bit of courage to do this, as the tortilla will still be quite wet, but if you take it carefully, everything will be fine. Cover the pan with a flat plate larger than the pan itself, then using thick oven gloves or tea towels to protect your hands, grasp both the pan and the plate and quickly turn them over so the tortilla is sitting on the plate, cooked-side up. Please don't worry if the top layer of egg runs quite a bit as you do this – it's hard to avoid and it won't make any difference to the finished dish. Add a splash more oil to the pan and slide the tortilla and any uncooked egg off the plate back into the pan to cook on the other side. Use the palette knife or a spatula to neatly tuck in the edges. Continue to cook the tortilla for a maximum of 3–4 minutes or until it's speckled golden on the bottom and firm but still moist. The ideal tortilla is lovely and tender in the centre.

We all need a Plan B! If you don't feel confident about turning the tortilla, don't worry; far rather be safe than sorry! Instead, preheat your grill to high heat and slide the whole pan (it will need to have a heatproof handle) under the grill until the top of the tortilla is set and feels just firm when lightly pressed.

When the tortilla is ready, gently slide it out of the pan onto a flat serving plate. Leave it to cool a little, as it tastes best when it's warm or at room temperature. Top with parsley leaves and serve with almond skordalia and a simple green salad (a ripe tomato, onion and olive salad with a sprinkle of basil leaves is lovely with it). Little wedges or squares make terrific finger food, too.

# Almond skordalia

MAKES 1 HEAPED CUP

about 120g stale pide
   (Turkish) bread
¼ cup (25g) almond meal
3 cloves garlic, finely chopped
¾ teaspoon sea salt flakes,
   or more to taste
½ cup (125ml) olive oil (I use
   a mixture of extra-virgin
   and regular), plus extra,
   for drizzling
1 tablespoon freshly squeezed
   lemon juice, or more to taste
parsley, dill or mint leaves,
   to garnish

Skordalia is like a thick, creamy and powerfully garlicky mayonnaise, and definitely not for the faint-hearted. Although to my mind, almost anything (well, anything within reason!) tastes better for a blob of this creamy, gloopy, garlicky stuff. It's fantastic with all sorts of barbecued seafood, great dolloped onto steamed veggies, or used as a healthy dip with carrot and cucumber sticks and celery stalks. The most important thing to remember when you make it is to use good, fresh garlic so you get a true, clear garlic flavour.

Remove the crusts from the pide bread and weigh it. You'll need 60g without crusts. Cut the bread into rough pieces and soak them in ¾ cup (180ml) cold water for 2 minutes only (any longer and the bread dissolves completely). Squeeze the soggy lumps of bread very tightly in your hands to get rid of the excess water – the bread will clump together into a mushy dough. Put this, along with the almond meal, garlic and salt, into a food processor fitted with the steel blade.

Now, this next stage of proceedings is the tricky bit about making skordalia. The secret to it is patience, for if the oil is added too rapidly, the mixture will split just like regular mayonnaise. Whiz everything together, then with the motor running, add the olive oil, drop by drop. As the mixture starts to come together you can increase the flow of oil to a very fine thread. The mixture should become very thick and creamy. About halfway through adding the oil, add the lemon juice and 1 tablespoon of boiling water (this will thin the skordalia down a bit). Continue adding the oil until it is all incorporated. Taste the skordalia and add a little more lemon juice, salt or boiling water to thin, if necessary.

I have to 'fess up that, from time to time, when I've been hurrying too much, I have added the oil too quickly and the skordalia has split. If the same thing should happen to you, I've found that immediately adding the lemon juice and boiling water can quite often salvage it. However, it may need more of each than the recipe says, in which case you will need to adjust the final texture and flavour.

Spoon the skordalia into a container, cover it tightly (very tightly, otherwise everything in the fridge will reek of garlic!) and store it in the fridge. Just prior to serving, scoop the skordalia into a serving bowl, sprinkle it with herb leaves and drizzle with extra-virgin olive oil. Store any leftover skordalia in an airtight container in the fridge for up to 6 days.

*Sunday 8ᵗʰ November*

# A classic ginger cake

When I drew the blinds earlier this morning, I was greeted by a veil of mist with a few rays of watery sunshine trying to filter through. It was dreamy and I couldn't help but go outside and watch as the sun burnt through the haze, revealing a world of spider webs sparkling with dew drops. They were everywhere, from tiny, absolutely perfect ones no bigger than my thumbnail to extraordinarily intricate cups, and multi-layered webs that would do an architect proud. In my fascination with them, I nearly missed seeing an exquisite emerald ground dove waddle solemnly across the lawn. Fortunately, he didn't realise I was there, and for a few minutes I sat spellbound, until in a flurry of astonishing emerald wings, he flew up into a tree. They're such beautiful birds and rarely seen. In moments like these, I feel incredibly blessed.

However, I can't afford to be too dreamy this morning. I really need to get my skates on as I have rather a lot of cooking to do today. First cab off the rank is a fragrant ginger cake. It's a recipe I've been working on for a long time and when I bought a hand of exquisite, pink-tipped young ginger at the market, this cake immediately sprang to mind. I know I can get a bit obsessive about recipes at times, and I guess I am with this one. Each time I make it, I tweak the ingredients just a little, trying to find that elusive perfect balance of spice and syrup that gives it its wonderful flavour and distinctive texture. My guess is that this is probably version number 17! And I must say, I'm pretty happy with it; the crumb is really light and studded with little chunks of glacé ginger, and the flavour is gingery but not overwhelmingly so. For me, to be quite perfect, it needs to be eaten with a dollop of cream (I think most ginger cakes benefit from this, it just softens the edges of the flavour and texture), but sans cream it still received the tick of approval from my Number One taste tester, so I figure I'm onto a winner!

*When I bought a hand of exquisite, pink-tipped young ginger at the market, this cake immediately sprang to mind.*

Happy Sunday. Belinda

# A classic ginger cake

SERVES 10–12

2 cups (300g) plain flour
1 tablespoon baking powder
1½ teaspoons ground
 cinnamon
1 teaspoon mixed spice
1 teaspoon ground ginger
¼ teaspoon freshly ground
 nutmeg
½ teaspoon salt
60g glacé ginger, very finely
 sliced, plus extra, finely
 sliced, to decorate
160g unsalted butter, at room
 temperature
¾ cup (175g) packed brown
 sugar
¾ cup (270g) golden syrup
¼ cup (80g) treacle
¼ cup (50g) finely grated
 fresh ginger
2 × 70g eggs
¾ cup (180g) sour cream,
 at room temperature
1½ teaspoons vanilla extract
finely grated zest of 1 lime
 (or lemon)
icing sugar, for dusting,
 optional
softly whipped cream,
 to serve, optional

I love that this cake uses three different forms of ginger – powdered, glacé, and fresh. Each adds its own distinctive flavour and makes the overall taste more complex and rounded.

Preheat your oven to 180°C. Butter a 22cm-square cake tin and line the base and sides with buttered baking paper. Set it aside.

Tip the flour, baking powder, cinnamon, mixed spice, ginger, nutmeg and salt into a bowl and whisk together for 1 minute with a balloon whisk so they're thoroughly aerated and combined. Add the ginger slices and toss them about so they're well coated in the flour mixture. Set the bowl aside.

Put the butter, brown sugar, golden syrup and treacle in the bowl of an electric mixer with the paddle attachment and beat them together on medium speed for about 4 minutes or until the mixture is very light and fluffy. Add the fresh ginger and mix until just combined. Add the eggs, one at a time, beating well after each addition. Now mix in the sour cream, vanilla and lime zest. If the batter starts to look curdled, add a few spoonfuls of the flour mixture. Finally, tip in the remaining flour mixture and combine it on low speed, but don't overdo this or the cake will be tough.

Scrape the batter into the prepared tin, spread it out evenly and decorate the top with the extra finely sliced glacé ginger. Pop the cake in the oven for 55 minutes–1 hour or until the centre springs back gently when pressed and a fine skewer inserted into the middle of the cake comes out clean.

Transfer the cake to a wire rack and leave it to cool in the tin for 15 minutes. After this time, sit another rack (or a plate) on top of the cake and quickly invert it onto this. Then sit the original wire rack on top and invert the cake again, so it's right-side up. Leave the cake to cool completely.

Carefully transfer the cake to a serving plate and dust with icing sugar, if using. Serve as is or with a dollop of cream. It keeps well in an airtight container (in fact, I find the flavour and texture improve) for at least 1 week.

*Sunday 15<sup>th</sup> November*

# Goat's cheese labne with cucumber and radish salad

I've just unmoulded the labne I made two days ago. This process has been on repeat these past few weeks, as the labne's refreshing tang and tartness have really helped lift our heat-jaded appetites. I wish you could see it! It looks so beautiful as it sits here in all its pristine glory – a perfect white dome, its surface textured by the muslin I used to drain it. I really can't tell you how much I love simple things like this – just looking at it makes me feel happy. For breakfast after our swim this morning, I'll scoop it onto plates, spoon a little honeycomb alongside and top it with grilled peaches. And tonight, I'm trying it instead of yoghurt in a bay leaf panna cotta. I'm also using it as a topping for crostini by mixing in a smidgen of prepared horseradish and loads of chopped dill and chives, then spooning it onto pumpernickel toasts and draping a morsel of smoked salmon on top. It's just one of those wonderfully versatile things to have on hand.

*It looks so beautiful as it sits here in all its pristine glory – a perfect white dome, its surface textured by muslin.*

Although labne is more often than not made solely with yoghurt, I quite often whisk in creamy marinated goat's cheese or feta before draining it to make it tangier and more savoury. It was when I was doing this that the idea for this salad occurred to me. What if I spread the labne down a long platter and spooned a refreshing salad of finely sliced cucumber, radish and mint over the top? How would that be? I like to think that the results speak for themselves. It's such an eye-catching but simple dish. We eat it slathered on slices of homemade pumpernickel bread, but warm flatbreads or Turkish pide bread would be wonderful, too. I'd love to think you get a chance to try it.

Happy Sunday. Belinda

# Goat's cheese labne with cucumber and radish salad

SERVES 6–8 (AS PART OF AN ANTIPASTI SPREAD)

250g trimmed radishes
(a variety of colours is lovely),
very finely sliced
260g small Lebanese
cucumbers
1½ tablespoons white wine
vinegar
1 tablespoon extra-virgin olive
oil, plus extra, for drizzling
1 teaspoon sea salt flakes
2 heaped tablespoons finely
chopped chives, or more
to taste
2 tablespoons finely shredded
mint leaves (dill is lovely, too)
a handful of small, whole mint
leaves or dill sprigs,
to garnish
crostini, pumpernickel bread
or warm flatbread, to serve

### GOAT'S CHEESE LABNE
180g marinated goat's cheese,
well drained
600g thick Greek-style
yoghurt
¼ teaspoon sea salt flakes

As my society garlic was flowering when we photographed this, I scattered some of its delicate mauve flowers on top of the dish, but herb leaves look really lovely, too.

For the labne, suspend a large-ish, fine sieve over a bowl, making sure that it doesn't touch the base. Line the sieve with a double layer of muslin, leaving an overhang all around.

Plop the goat's cheese into a medium-size bowl and mash it with a potato masher to make it as smooth as possible, then give it a good stir. Add a large dollop of yoghurt to the bowl and thoroughly whisk it into the goat's cheese (a balloon whisk is helpful here). Add another dollop of yoghurt and do the same again, then add the remainder along with the salt and mix everything together until the mixture is smooth.

Scoop the yoghurt mixture into the muslin-lined sieve, then draw the muslin up over the top of it, pressing down gently. Cover the whole lot with beeswax wrap or cling film and pop it in the fridge for 24 hours. The next day, discard the liquid that's collected in the bowl (there's a surprising amount). I use the labne at this stage; however, if you'd like it to be firmer, you can cover it and leave it to drain in the fridge for another day.

Just before serving, pop the radish into a bowl. Peel half the cucumbers and slice them thinly, too. Lastly, slice the remaining cucumbers with their skins on, then add both lots to the bowl with the radish. Drizzle the vinegar and 1 tablespoon of olive oil over the top. Sprinkle with the sea salt, chives and shredded mint leaves, then use very clean hands (or don a pair of prep gloves) to gently mix the salad together. It's best to do this at the last minute, otherwise the cucumber tends to weep and dilute the dressing.

To serve, roughly spread the labne over the base of a serving platter. Drizzle a little olive oil lightly over the top, then pile the salad on top of the labne, making sure some labne peeks out around the edges. Scatter over a handful of mint leaves or dill sprigs. The idea is to scoop some of the labne onto crostini, pumpernickel bread or warm flatbread and eat it with the salad.

# Fragrant spiced chicken with minted yoghurt

And just like that, this topsy turvy year in the cooking school has ended. As always, our day slowly wound to a halt. First, our lovely participants departed with smiles and waves, clutching their recipes and goodie bags. Next, we farewelled our two wonderful and ultra-talented helpers, Belle and Laura, who work so hard to keep everything in the kitchen flowing smoothly – washing dishes, answering questions (they're both fabulous cooks), and helping everyone, including keeping an eye out for Clive and me. I can't thank you both enough.

Then there was just the two of us. As we swept, mopped and quietly packed up a year of memories into boxes, we reminisced about all that had occurred these past months within the walls of this lovely, old hall. The highs and lows, the laughter and tears, the friendships forged and, of course, the dishes cooked and shared. Finally, it was our turn to depart. We switched off the lights, bade farewell to the resident possum (and begged him not to fall through the ceiling again in our absence), and took our leave of the cows as they meandered their way back to the paddock after milking. Then we, too, turned for home with weary bodies but full hearts.

On that note, I'll say goodbye for the kettle has yet to be boiled and I'm badly in need of that first welcome cup of tea! But I thought you might like to try this lovely spicy chicken recipe, as it has been one of our most popular dishes at the cooking school this year.

Happy Sunday. Belinda ♥

*As we swept, mopped and quietly packed a year of memories into boxes, we reminisced over all that had occurred within the walls of this lovely, old hall.*

## Fragrant spiced chicken with minted yoghurt

SERVES 8

8 chicken thigh cutlets
    (bone-in, skin-on chicken
    thighs, sometimes called
    chicken 'chops')
coriander leaves, to garnish
lime (or lemon) cheeks,
    to serve

**CHICKEN MARINADE**
⅔ cup (160ml) extra-virgin
    olive oil
finely grated zest of 1 lemon
2 tablespoons freshly
    squeezed lemon juice
2 large cloves garlic, finely
    chopped
1 tablespoon smoked paprika
1 tablespoon ground cumin
1 tablespoon ground coriander
    seeds
1 teaspoon ground turmeric
1 teaspoon cinnamon
½–1 teaspoon dried chilli
    flakes, or more to taste
⅓ cup (a large handful)
    chopped coriander leaves
1–2 teaspoons sea salt flakes
freshly ground black pepper,
    to taste

**MINTED YOGHURT**
1½ cups (420g) thick
    Greek-style yoghurt
1½ teaspoons freshly ground
    cumin, or more to taste, plus
    extra, to finish
very large handful mint leaves,
    finely shredded
splash of extra-virgin olive oil,
    plus extra, to finish
1 teaspoon sea salt flakes,
    or more to taste
mint leaves, to garnish,
    optional

Put all the chicken marinade ingredients into a large bowl and give them a thorough stir to make a paste. Add the chicken cutlets and swish them about so they're really well coated in the marinade (it's a good idea to don a pair of prep gloves and do this with your hands, as this way you can really work the paste into the chook without dyeing your fingers a rather startling shade of orange!). Line a container that will hold the chicken comfortably with a plastic bag. Pile the chicken into the bag, scrape in any leftover marinade as well, then knot the bag tightly. Seal the container and pop it in the fridge for at least 5 hours or, preferably, overnight (the longer you leave the chicken, the more imbued it will become with the spices). Give the bag a good squish occasionally.

When you're ready to cook the chicken, preheat your oven to 190°C.

Line a large, shallow baking tray with foil, then baking paper. Sit the chicken cutlets in the tray, skin-side up, in a single layer. Make sure the chicken is well coated in the marinade. Pop the tray in the oven and roast the chicken for about 40 minutes or until it's deep-brown and cooked through but tender.

While the chicken is cooking, make the minted yoghurt. Simply combine all the ingredients, except the mint leaves to garnish, in a bowl and thoroughly mix them together. Taste it and add more of anything you like – salt, oil, mint or cumin, whatever makes it taste just right to you. Scrape the mixture into a small serving bowl, cover it and pop it in the fridge. Just prior to serving, drizzle it with a tiny bit of extra olive oil and sprinkle with a bit more cumin to finish. Scatter over a few mint leaves, if using.

Transfer the chicken to a serving platter and spoon a little of the cooking juices over the top. Garnish with coriander leaves and serve with lime cheeks and the minted yoghurt.

# Dark chocolate, caramelised date and hazelnut brownies

It's funny, really, I can give or take chocolate biscuits and cakes much of the time, but I find it hard to go past a chocolate brownie. However, that said, it has to be a *really* good brownie – fudgy and gooey inside with a delicate, papery surface, and texture that dissolves on my tongue. The trouble is, they're not all that easy to come by. More often than not, they just don't have the beautiful melt-in-the-mouth quality that I'm after. Over time, I've made many variations of them trying to nail the elusive perfect proportions of butter, chocolate and eggs. But, funnily enough, still my all-time favourite is one of the earliest I worked on and I think I've had more compliments about it than pretty much any other recipe of mine! It has just the right balance of everything to give it the most beautiful, velvety texture, while little chunks of hazelnut add a lovely crunch – and it's a breeze to make. This is my latest take on it and, I have to say, I'm really happy with it. The brownie is enhanced with dollops of caramelised date paste, which give it a whole other dimension – slightly stickier and gooey-er and with a lovely caramel back note. But if you just want a plain one, you can leave the date mixture out. I guess I don't need to say that it's rich and probably best eaten in small morsels, but that goes hand-in-hand with brownies, doesn't it?

Happy Sunday. Belinda 🖤

*I find it hard to go past a good chocolate brownie, but it has to be really good – fudgy and gooey inside with a delicate, papery surface, and texture that dissolves on my tongue.*

# Dark chocolate, caramelised date and hazelnut brownie

MAKES 12–14

90g roasted hazelnuts
  (see note, opposite page)
¼ cup (35g) plain flour
  (spelt flour is fine)
¼ teaspoon baking powder
¼ teaspoon salt
225g good-quality dark
  chocolate, roughly chopped
⅔ cup (150g) caster sugar
180g unsalted butter
  at room temperature
2 × 60g eggs
3 teaspoons vanilla extract
120g good-quality dark
  chocolate, extra, chopped
  into small pieces
icing sugar, for dusting,
  optional

## CARAMELISED DATE PASTE

⅓ cup (75g) caster sugar
125g pitted dates, coarsely
  chopped
2 tablespoons crème fraîche
  (or sour cream or pure
  cream)
½–¾ teaspoon fig or balsamic
  vinegar, or more to taste

For the caramelised date paste, put the sugar and 2 tablespoons of water into a small, heavy-based saucepan over medium heat and stir until the sugar has dissolved. Once dissolved, stop stirring, increase the heat and bring the mixture to the boil. Allow it to boil, undisturbed, washing down the sides of the pan occasionally with a brush dipped in water to remove any sugar crystals that may form. Once the syrup turns light amber, watch it like a hawk – you want it to become a gorgeous, rich brown, but not so dark that it burns. When it's ready, remove the pan from the heat and stir in the dates and crème fraîche. (Be mindful to protect your hands with long oven gloves or thick tea towels when you do this, as it may well spit a bit.) Cover the pan and leave the mixture to cool for 15 minutes, then stir in the vinegar. Finally, mash it with a potato masher or balloon whisk to form a chunky paste, then set it aside.

Preheat your oven to 160°C. Butter a 22cm-square cake tin and line the base and sides with overlapping sheets of buttered baking paper, leaving an overhang all around to stop the brownie sticking and to act as handles to help ease it out of the tin. Set it aside.

Pulse the hazelnuts in a food processor fitted with the steel blade to chop them coarsely. Tip them into a bowl and toss them with a couple of teaspoons of the flour. Set the bowl aside.

Whiz the remaining flour, baking powder and salt in the processor until they're just combined, then tip them into another bowl. Now add the 225g roughly chopped dark chocolate and the sugar to the processor and whiz them together until the chocolate is very finely chopped. Add the butter, eggs and vanilla extract to the chocolate mixture and whiz them together for 1 minute, stopping to scrape down the sides once or twice with a spatula. Add the flour mixture and pulse only until everything just combines into a thick batter. Use a spatula to stir in the hazelnuts and small chocolate pieces, then smooth the batter into the prepared tin. Dot the top evenly with heaped teaspoonsful of the caramelised date paste (if the paste has hardened too much, just warm it gently to be able to spoon it up).

Bake the brownie for about 40 minutes or until a wooden toothpick inserted into the middle comes out with moist, but not wet, crumbs on it. Cool the brownie in the tin on a wire rack. Once it's cool, pop it in the fridge to chill.

To cut the brownie, use the overhanging paper to ease it out of the tin. Invert it onto a flat plate and gently peel away the paper, then invert it again onto a chopping board. Slice the brownie into bars with a hot, dry knife. Before serving the bars, return them to cool room temperature, then dust with icing sugar to give them pretty, snowy tops. Layer the remaining bars between sheets of baking paper in an airtight container. Store them in the fridge for 10 days or so (or freeze them for up to 4 weeks).

### A NOTE ON ROASTING YOUR OWN HAZELNUTS

Although you can buy roasted hazelnuts, it's very simple to do your own and they taste so much fresher and sweeter. Just spread the shelled nuts (they will still have their dark skins) onto a shallow baking tray. Pop the tray in a 180°C oven and roast the nuts for about 10 minutes or until the skins have darkened and started to split.

When they're ready, remove from the oven, then immediately tip them into a clean tea towel. Bundle the nuts up in the towel and leave them for a few minutes to sweat. Now, twist the tea towel tightly so it forms a pouch enclosing the nuts and bang it on the bench to help loosen the skins (it takes a while to do this, so be patient). Open up the tea towel, scoop up a small handful of nuts and rub them vigorously in the palms of your hands to loosen and remove the skins. Don't worry if they still have some bits of skin clinging stubbornly to them; it's nearly impossible to remove it all.

# DECEMBER

Chicken, smoked cheese and bacon rotolo

Bircher muesli with roasted plums, apricots and blueberries

Classic ginger petticoat tails

Charred eggplant and ginger dip

Brown rice and sesame crackers

# Chicken, smoked cheese and bacon rotolo

Every Christmas I think to myself how lovely it would be to do something different on Christmas Day. "Let's take prawn sandwiches and mangoes to the beach, find a shady spot, and spend the day there," I say, brightly, only to be met by deafening silence. "We could just have a really nice brunch and then spend the rest of the day watching old movies, going for swims and eating mince pies?" I suggest. Stony silence this time. "What about changing what we usually eat then? That might be fun?" A slightly more positive response to this, but not for long. "Yes, we could do that, but you will make your lentil salad, won't you? I know duck would be nice for a change, but we'll still have the ham, too, won't we?" It doesn't take long for me to completely give in and repeat the menu we so often have, which consists of a glass of Champagne with homemade cheese biscuits and warm olives (my niece would never forgive me if we didn't have her favourite 'olivers'), glazed ham with rhubarb chutney and hot English mustard, herb-roasted chickens, lentil or sweet potato salad (I'm allowed a little leeway here, but only as long as the dressing is the same ☺), potato salad for my darling husband (his absolute favourite), and a green salad from whatever's in the garden. All this to be followed by a family-size fruit mince pie, dusted with icing sugar and served with homemade cinnamon ice-cream and custard.

*It's rather grand and festive and very Christmassy. The lovely thing about it is that we can eat it warm on Christmas Day and then have leftovers for a picnic.*

Actually, truth be told, I don't mind cooking the same meal at all. I realise how important family rituals, big and small, are in our lives. And I can hardly talk, as I'm the girl who gets out my childhood Santa sack, my name stencilled on it in Mum's lovely writing, and put it, not on the end of my bed now, but under the tree to bring a part of her to our celebration, too. That said, this year I've suggested one rather significant change, which after a lot of umming and aahing, has been somewhat grudgingly allowed. That's because there are fewer of us now, so we can replace the ham and chicken with this lovely rotolo, which combines both these things in a totally different way. It's rather grand and festive and very Christmassy. The best thing about it is that we can eat it warm on Christmas Day and then have leftovers for a Boxing Day picnic. I'm determined to get that picnic in somewhere!

Happy Sunday. Belinda 💙

## Chicken, smoked cheese and bacon rotolo

SERVES 8–10

1kg chicken mince (or pork and veal mince, or a mixture, if you would rather)
150g your favourite classic salami, diced
2 onions, finely chopped
2 cloves garlic, finely chopped
1½ tablespoons Dijon mustard
1 teaspoon hot English mustard powder
1 teaspoon sea salt flakes
2 tablespoons finely grated parmesan cheese
1 tablespoon chopped thyme leaves
½ cup coarsely chopped flat-leaf parsley
2 × 60g eggs, lightly beaten
¼ cup (60ml) milk
2 cups (140g) fresh white breadcrumbs (a good, firm sourdough loaf is ideal)
1 bunch mint, leaves picked
6 large thin slices leg ham
150g smoked cheese (smoked mozzarella is ideal), grated
10 large rashers bacon, rinds removed
small bunch of bay leaves or other herb sprigs, to garnish

Line a large baking tray with baking paper and set it aside.

Put the mince, salami, onion, garlic, Dijon mustard, mustard powder, salt, parmesan, thyme, and parsley into a large bowl and mix them thoroughly together. The best way to make sure that everything is evenly mixed is to do this by hand, either with clean hands or wearing prep gloves.

In another bowl, whisk together the eggs and milk. Pour this mixture into the mince mixture and combine it well, then tip in the breadcrumbs and mix them in thoroughly. Pop the mixture in the fridge for 30 minutes to chill.

Scoop the mixture onto a large sheet of baking paper and pat it out into an even 40cm × 30cm rectangle, making sure a long side is facing you (I usually draw an outline of the rectangle on the baking paper so I get the size right). Press mint leaves all over the surface, then slightly overlap the ham slices on top. Sprinkle the grated cheese in a 10cm-wide band down the middle, parallel to the longest sides.

Using the baking paper underneath as an aid and starting from the long side nearest you, carefully roll up the mixture like a jam roll, peeling back the paper as you go. On the final roll, slide the loaf, seam-side down, off the paper onto the prepared baking tray. Use your hands to neaten it up if it has bulged a little. Arrange the bacon rashers crosswise over the loaf, overlapping them slightly and tucking the ends underneath (you'll need to trim the bacon to fit – I use the off-cuts to patch any gaps). Put the rotolo in the fridge for 30 minutes to firm up a little.

Preheat your oven to 180°C. Pop the tray in the oven and bake the rotolo for 1 hour. If the bacon isn't as golden as you would like at the end of the cooking time and you have a grill in your oven, you can slide the tray with the rotolo under a hot grill for a couple of minutes to colour it a little more.

When it's ready, remove the rotolo from the oven and leave it to settle for at least 20 minutes before slicing. With the help of the baking paper and a long, wide palette knife or spatula, carefully wiggle it off the paper and onto a long serving platter. It looks lovely served partly sliced and garnished with a bunch of bay leaves or herb sprigs.

# Bircher muesli with roasted plums, apricots and blueberries

From when I was a little girl, I've been an early morning swimmer. Before school in summer I would walk down to the beach with my brother and cousin, feeling awfully proud of myself as I was allowed to body surf with the 'big boys'. They taught me so much (although, I suspect my mum would've been horrified if she had seen the size of the waves they took me out in!). These memories come flooding back at this time of year when the Christmas and New Year king tides sweep in, bringing that clear, icy water I remember so well. This morning was no exception when we went for an early dip to cool ourselves down after an unbearably sticky night. Honestly, to dive into that familiar frigid water was absolute heaven. I swear there was a hiss of steam as our hot bodies sank below the surface!

Of course, now we're back home from our swim and absolutely ravenous (what is it about saltwater and sunshine that creates such an appetite?). So we're about to sit outside on the deck, still in our cossies, and tuck into bowls of homemade bircher muesli topped with roasted apricots and plums, and thick yoghurt – they're the simplest recipes and ones I make constantly.

*To dive into that familiar frigid water was absolute heaven. I swear there was a hiss of steam as our hot bodies sank below the surface!*

For the roasted fruit, simply halve and stone about half-a-dozen apricots and plums (or one or the other, if that's all you can find), and sit them cut-side up in 1–2 large, shallow ovenproof dishes (a large gratin dish is ideal). Mix together about ¾ cup (180ml) maple syrup with 1 teaspoon of vanilla extract, and trickle it evenly over the fruit. Pop the dish in a very hot oven (230°C) for 12–15 minutes or until the juices are bubbling and the plums and apricots are tender, then remove and let the fruit cool. That's it! The high heat and sweet syrup intensify the flavours of the fruit and they're extraordinarily delicious. I cooked the ones we're about to eat just before we left for our swim, so they're still a little warm and all the better and more luscious for being so, I'd have to say. The bircher muesli recipe follows, and is a staple for us during summer.

Happy Sunday. Belinda ♥

## Bircher muesli with roasted plums, apricots and blueberries

SERVES 6

2½ cups (225g) traditional rolled oats
80g natural sultanas
90g roasted pecans or macadamias, coarsely chopped
1½ cups (375ml) soy milk (or regular milk)
1 cup (280g) thick natural yoghurt
2 small apples, grated
a smidgen of honey, optional
roasted plums and apricots (see recipe, previous page)
a handful of blueberries, optional

Put the oats, sultanas and nuts into a bowl and stir them together. Add the soy milk, yoghurt and 1 cup (250ml) water, and thoroughly mix them together. Cover the bowl and pop it in the fridge overnight for the oats to absorb the liquid.

Just before serving the bircher muesli, stir in the grated apple and honey, if using. Spoon it into bowls and top with the roasted fruit and a smattering of blueberries. Any leftover bircher muesli keeps really well in the fridge for up to 5 days.

*Sunday 20th December*

# Classic ginger petticoat tails

My sister arrives this afternoon. Her arrival heralds my favourite time of all in this hectic festive week – the decorating of the Christmas tree. Well, it's not really a tree. More a collection of bare branches and twigs cut from our lilly pilly, many already festooned in delicate lichen. It's a ritual for us. We sit on the floor, a tray of tea things beside us, and unpack the decorations, sorting and sifting through them, telling stories and reminiscing as we go. The teapot empties and is refilled, our hands working constantly as we hang, garland, and string tiny lights along the branches, standing back every so often to see the effect. My heart settles as we talk, the busyness of the past weeks melts away, and a sense of calm begins to prevail, at last.
Of course, all our chat and decorating is fuelled by the Christmas cake – my sister's favourite Christmas treat and something I always have ready for her arrival. And my favourite thing of all – buttery, ginger-studded shortbread. If I make nothing else at Christmas, these two are non-negotiable.

The shortbread isn't only for us; it makes such a special gift that I always try to bake extra. I know how much I love to be given something homemade, and I feel sure that others do, too. Occasionally, I make it in rounds like the one here, with markings traditionally known as petticoat tails. There are all sorts of theories as to how they came by their name, but the one I like most is that the shape resembles the full, bell-hoop crinolines that women once wore – thank goodness we don't now!

Happy Sunday before Christmas! Belinda 🖤

*The teapot empties and is refilled, and our hands work constantly as we hang, garland, and string tiny lights around the branches.*

# Classic ginger petticoat tails

MAKES 1 ROUND
(OR 12 PETTICOAT TAILS)

225g unsalted butter, at cool
  room temperature
½ cup (110g) caster sugar
2 cups (300g) plain flour
¼ teaspoon salt
60g (about 10 chunks)
  crystallised or glacé ginger,
  very finely chopped,
  plus extra, finely sliced,
  to decorate
2 teaspoons white sugar,
  for sprinkling

Put a 23cm loose-based tart tin into the fridge to chill.

Scrape the butter into the bowl of an electric mixer fitted with the paddle attachment and beat it for 2 minutes on medium–high speed. Add the caster sugar, a little at a time, and once it's all incorporated, beat the mixture for about 3 minutes until it's light and fluffy.

Reduce the speed to low and sprinkle in 1 cup (150g) flour and the salt. Once this is absorbed, slowly shake in the remaining flour and mix until it's combined, stopping and scraping down the sides of the bowl occasionally. Finally, sprinkle in the finely chopped ginger and stop the machine as soon as it's incorporated. Scrape the dough into the chilled tart tin, patting it down gently to get it as even as possible, then roll a small jar or tumbler over the top to help level the surface. If you like, press the tines of a fork around the edge to form a decorative border, then rest a ruler across the top of the pan and use it as a guide to score the round into 12 even wedges with the point of a small sharp knife. Finally, prick each wedge a few times with the fork. Cover and chill the shortbread for at least 2 hours (you can leave it like this for 1–2 days before baking).

Preheat your oven to 155°C. Press a slice of the extra sliced ginger onto each marked wedge and sprinkle the whole round lightly with the white sugar. Bake for 1¼–1½ hours until the shortbread is pale golden. Remove the tin to a wire rack and leave the shortbread to cool for 5 minutes. Then, while it's still quite hot, use the ruler again as a guide to gently cut all the way through the score marks you made previously. Leave the shortbread to cool completely in the tin.

Store the wedges in airtight containers, layered between baking paper, or wrap the whole round as a gift. One of the really nice things about this shortbread is that, as long as the container is airtight, it keeps well for up to 1 month and improves in flavour.

## TO MAKE SHORTBREAD FINGERS

Once you've made the dough, pat it out to form a 1cm-thick rectangle. I don't mind the slightly wonky edges, but you can use a pastry or dough scraper to neaten the edges, if you like. Score it into fingers, prick and chill it as above.

When you're ready to bake the shortbread, cut through the score marks to create fingers, then space them out on 1–2 baking trays lined with baking paper. Pop them in the oven and bake the shortbread fingers, rotating the trays now and then so they colour evenly, for 45–50 minutes or until pale golden. Cool on the tray. You'll find the fingers tend to be crisper, as the dough is not as compacted as it is in the tin.

# Charred eggplant and ginger dip with brown rice and sesame crackers

It's hard to believe that another year is coming to an end. I remember my mum, Cooee, saying to me many years ago that the years just seemed to fly by the older she became. I don't think I really understood what she meant until the age I am now, where a year seems to pass in the blink of an eye. As a child it seemed an eternity until summer school holidays or my birthday arrived, yet now they come around alarmingly quickly.

I suspect our New Year's Eve will be spent quietly with a few close friends, having a simple meal, chatting and laughing. We'll be tucked up in bed by 10pm, which is late for the country, believe me! Although, if past years are any indicator, once everyone has gone and we've cleaned up, we'll take a glass of wine out onto the deck and sit quietly in the still and dark, drinking in the fragrance of the night-flowering jasmine and letting the night wash over us. I love summer evenings like this, when the air is balmy and soft, the fruit bats are squabbling in the melaleucas, and the Milky Way sparkles overhead as though a giant has scattered a zillion diamonds across the sky. The wonder of it all sinks in and my sense of gratitude to be here in this world and experience all this fills me to the brim. It's a beautiful way to say goodbye to, and acknowledge, all that has occurred in the year just passed, and to look forward to the year to come.

These lovely eggplant dip and brown rice cracker recipes have been a constant on our table through this festive season. I hope you enjoy them. And I hope that however you spend this New Year's Eve, it heralds the start of a year filled with kindness, peace and good health.

Happy New Year! Belinda 🖤

*The wonder of it all sinks in and my sense of gratitude to be here and experience all this fills me to the brim.*

## Charred eggplant and ginger dip

SERVES 4-6

750g (about 2 large-ish) firm, shiny-skinned eggplants
¼ cup (60g) tahini
1 smallish clove garlic, very finely chopped
½-1 teaspoon finely chopped fresh ginger, or more to taste
2½ tablespoons (50ml) freshly squeezed lemon juice
1 tablespoon extra-virgin olive oil, plus extra, for drizzling
½ teaspoon sesame oil
1½ teaspoons sea salt flakes, or more to taste
small herb leaves or spray-free edible flowers, to garnish

Preheat your barbecue to high, then sit a wire rack over a plate and set it aside.

Prick each eggplant about a dozen times with a fine skewer, then sit them on the barbecue. If your barbecue has a lid, close it. Otherwise, upturn a large, stainless-steel bowl over the eggplants to mimic a lid. Cook them, turning regularly with tongs, for 25–30 minutes or until the skin has blistered and blackened all over. The eggplants will have collapsed in on themselves and look rather unprepossessing, and the flesh will feel really soft when you give it a gentle prod (smaller eggplants will take less time to cook).

Remove the eggplants to the wire rack and leave them for 15 minutes or until they're cool enough to handle. Halve the eggplants lengthwise and drain any liquid that pools around them. Use a spoon to scrape the creamy flesh from the charred skin, then plop it into a medium-size bowl and mash it with a fork or potato masher to form a chunky puree.

Add the tahini, garlic, ginger and lemon juice to the bowl and thoroughly mix everything together with a spoon. Finally, use the spoon to beat in the olive oil, sesame oil and salt – the mixture will become lighter and fluffier as you do this. Taste the eggplant and adjust the flavours to suit you. Set the bowl aside in a cool spot (by the way, this keeps well in the fridge for up to 5 days).

Scoop the eggplant dip into a serving bowl, drizzle over a little extra olive oil and garnish with a sprinkle of herb leaves or flowers. Serve with the brown rice and sesame crackers (see recipe, below).

## Brown rice and sesame crackers

MAKES 26-30 CRACKERS

¾ cup (170g) organic short grain brown rice (to yield 2 cups cooked)
¼ cup (45g) organic golden linseeds (flaxseeds)
¼ cup (40g) organic sesame seeds
¼ cup (40g) organic chia seeds
1½ teaspoons sea salt flakes

As so many people I know are trying to avoid gluten, I find myself experimenting more and more with gluten-free cakes and biscuits, as they're the things that everyone seems to miss the most. I must admit I have become rather addicted to these crackers since I first tried them. They're fun to make, extremely more-ish, and perhaps my all-time favourite for scooping up hummus. I use organic seeds, but if you can't find organic, it doesn't matter at all.

Bring a large saucepan of lightly salted water to the boil, then add the rice. Give it a good stir, then adjust the heat so the rice bubbles steadily. Cook the rice for about 30 minutes or until it's tender (timing will depend on the rice you use). As soon as it's ready, drain the rice through a fine sieve. Give the sieve a couple of firm taps to remove any excess water, then sit it over a bowl and leave the rice to cool.

Preheat your oven to 180°C. Have 2 large-ish baking sheets on hand and measure out 4 sheets of baking paper to fit them.

Measure out 2 cups of cooked rice (there may be a little leftover for another use) and tip it into a food processor fitted with the steel blade. Add the linseeds, sesame seeds, chia seeds and salt and whiz the mixture together until it forms a squishy ball around the blade (many of the seeds will still be whole, but the rice will be reduced to a mush). If it won't form a ball, trickle in a tiny splash of cold water and whiz again to help bring it together.

Scrape half the mixture into the middle of a sheet of baking paper. Lightly moisten your hands and shape the mixture into a rough rectangle running lengthwise up your sheet. Sit another sheet of baking paper on top and press down quite firmly to flatten it a bit. Now use a rolling pin to roll the mixture out as thinly as you can. Carefully transfer the whole thing to a baking sheet. Repeat this with the remaining mixture and baking paper.

Put the baking sheets in the oven and bake for 15 minutes. Remove the sheets from the oven and, using a broad-bladed spatula or egg slice and your fingers, lift off and discard the top sheet of baking paper and carefully turn the now partly firm cracker mixture over – this is easier than it sounds! Don't worry if it breaks a bit, it will be fine. Return the sheets to the oven and bake the crackers for another 12 minutes – they will start to get a pale-gold tinge and smell nutty and delicious. Remove the baking sheets from the oven again and use a knife or your fingers to break the cracker sheets into pieces the size you would like. Just a word of warning here, this is a bit tricky as the cracker mixture is really hot, so please be careful. Return the baking sheets to the oven and cook the crackers for another 8–10 minutes or until they're pale golden in parts and crisp. (Just be mindful that some pieces may be a bit thinner than others, so keep an eye on them and remove them as they're ready.)

Carefully transfer the crackers to a wire rack and leave them to cool completely. Store them in an airtight jar – they should keep well for up to 1 week. Serve with the charred eggplant and ginger dip.

# Index

# Thank you

There have been a number of wonderful people who have helped this book come about and I'm immensely grateful to each and every one of you.

First and foremost, thank you to Julie Gibbs, the publisher of all eight of my books and a dear friend, whose inquisitive mind and unfailing enthusiasm and support always inspires me and pushes me out of my comfort zone. I'll never forget the sparkle in your eyes when we first discussed this book – thank you so much for running with it! I also owe a big thanks to Dan Ruffino, managing director of Simon & Schuster, and a very enthusiastic supporter of this somewhat unusual project. Thank you, too, to Anna O'Grady and Angus Dalton, from the extraordinarily talented marketing and publicity team at Simon & Schuster. It has been a real pleasure to work with you both.

My lovely editor, Lara Picone, you're a gem, and have remained steady, calm and focused throughout what has been a very hectic schedule. Thank you.

Katrina O'Brien, what a delight it has been to have you come on board for yet another of my books. Thank you for so much for your keen eye and gentle understanding.

I was thrilled to bits when I heard you were to design this book, Daniel New, as I've always been a great fan – it's as quirky and beautiful as I had hoped it could be.

Rodney, my old friend, can you believe we have worked together for more than 30 years now! I've loved every minute of our time together and remain in awe of your unfailing eye and the beauty of your photographs. It has been an unexpected joy to work with you on yet another book.

Thank you to my lovely sister and stylist, Cass Stokes, whose unerring eye for just the right plate, platter or bowl to complement the dishes I cook is totally invaluable. I love working with you. Thank you, too, to those who helped you; Mud Australia for your beautiful ceramics, and Major & Tom for such wonderful props.

It was such a delight to use ceramics from two lovely local potters, Jo Norton and Jenn Johnston. So much of this book is about local produce and where we live, so your gorgeous handcrafted ware was a perfect match.

Our cooking school wouldn't be nearly so lovely without the support of Fackelmann Housewares. Thank you for your ongoing generosity, we're really proud to use your beautiful kitchen and tableware.

I'm hugely grateful to the generous-spirited local farmers and producers from the Mullumbimby Farmers Market. What you do inspires and informs everything I do, thank you.

As ever, my much-loved family and friends have helped me through the very intense schedule that a book such as this requires. Thank you so much for your understanding and kindness when I disappeared down the rabbit hole! Especially you, Clive, with your unerring love, patience and endless support. If you weren't by my side, I suspect I would most certainly still be washing dishes from the shoot!

And last, but most definitely not least, the biggest thank you of all is to you, my lovely followers on Instagram, without your comments and encouragement this book simply wouldn't have come about. Thank you from the bottom of my heart.

Belinda 🖤

# About the author

Belinda lives, cooks and teaches in the beautiful Byron
Bay hinterland – a region known for its bountiful farmers
markets. It's these markets and the produce in them that
informs and inspires the dishes she cooks. She has a
wonderful knack for creating recipes for food you genuinely
want to eat, and a warm, distinctive writing style, which
makes you feel as though she is standing beside you in the
kitchen as you cook (one of the most oft heard comments
about her books). This award-winning author has worked
as a chef, TV food presenter, freelance writer, restaurant
reviewer and cooking teacher. Belinda's books include *Belinda
Jeffery's Collected Recipes; Mix & Bake; The Country Cook
Book*; *Desserts*; the immensely popular *Utterly Delicious
Simple Food;* and *The Salad Book.*

A YEAR OF SUNDAYS
First published in Australia in 2021 by
Simon & Schuster (Australia) Pty Limited
Suite 19A, Level 1, Building C, 450 Miller Street, Cammeray, NSW 2062

A JULIE GIBBS BOOK
for

SIMON & SCHUSTER
AUSTRALIA

10 9 8 7 6 5 4 3 2 1

Sydney New York London Toronto New Delhi
Visit our website at simonandschuster.com.au

NATIONAL
LIBRARY
OF AUSTRALIA

A catalogue record for this
book is available from the
National Library of Australia

ISBN: 9781761102189

Publisher: Julie Gibbs
Photographer: Rodney Weidland
Designer and illustrator: Daniel New
Typesetter: Hannah Schubert
Editor: Lara Picone
Printed and bound in China by Asia Pacific Offset Limited

FSC
www.fsc.org

MIX
Paper from
responsible sources
FSC® C136333